FORWARD

Some stories are too painful not to tell. They show how the soul fared when problems afflicted, and circumstances disrupted what it intended for itself. In this regard, Sharilyn's book paints a revealing picture of the power of emotions and the need for decisions that enable us to reclaim ourselves personally, spiritually, and psychologically. Each is important because they reveal patterns we overlook and practices we permit that often sabotage what we set for ourselves. Her transparency teaches, and her authenticity reaches across classes, races, and religions.

If you've ever suffered trauma and felt like your life was over, read this book! You will be strengthened, enlightened, and encouraged.

Dr. Joel Bryant, Ed.D.

DNA'S Truth Her Nightmare His Blessing
Copyright © 2024 Sharilyn W. Belinfante

All rights reserved. No part of this publication may be reproduced, distributed, or transmitted in any form or by any means, including photocopying, recording, or other electronic or mechanical methods, without the prior written permission of the author or publisher, except in the case of brief quotations embodied in critical reviews and certain other noncommercial uses permitted by copyright law. For permission requests, write to the publisher, addressed "Attention: Permissions Coordinator," at the email address below.

Any references to historical events, real people, or places are fictitious. Names, characters, and places are products of the author's imagination.

Publisher: Calm Expressions Publishing
www.ebonystubbs.com

ISBN: 979-8-9916974-0-8 (Paperback)

Printed by Create Space., in the United States of America.

Acknowledgment

I thank God for the opportunity to write this book and everyone who has contributed to its creation.

Special thanks to Dr. Barbara Y. James for encouraging me to start and to get it finished.

Dr. Joel Bryant for his knowledge and critiques.

And a special thanks to my kingdom sister, Mia Roan Brooks, for the long hours she spent with me and the time she gave out of her busy days to make this book readable.

I am eternally grateful.

Dedication

This book is dedicated to the Lover of my soul, my first husband. The Lord of hosts, the King of kings, the Holy One of Israel, He is called the God of the whole earth, Abba.

And to the memory of my mother, Bernadine James.

Also, to the silent ones who long for family and true identity.

DNA'S TRUTH

Her Nightmare

His Blessing
Owner

SWBelinfante77@gmail.com

Contents

The Promise 6

Introduction 7

Formative Years 10

The Relationship 22

Show and Tell...35

I'll Be There 46

The Next Day..55

Summer Vacation 66

Lost and Found 77

New Birth 100

Sharmeka Lee 119

The Questions 129

Reunited Feeling Good 138

Red Ants 155

Sisters..163

Love's Blanket 169

The Nightmare 177

The Blessing 190

The Promise

As I laid my head beside Mother's on the hospital bed while she was leaving this life for the next, I told her I would write our story. She believed it would make a good Lifetime movie. We loved watching them together.

It has been too many years since I made that promise; I cannot let any more time pass without fulfilling it, so here we go, our story.

Introduction

In the silence of the night, when all had laid to rest, the sounds of the night were loud. It was like a symphony, and each creature knew when to come in with its unique sound. The wind blew at the right moment to allow the ruffling of the leaves and branches of the trees to make their applause.

The woods were dark. If not for the bright moonlight, Deanna would not have been able to see her hand in front of her face, but she could see the path clearly as she walked through the vast thickness towards the river. The river was nearby, yet it seemed so far away this night, thought Deanna.

Deanna walked slow and steady, feeling the dampness of the night's dew against her feet and legs from the grass and small bushes.

Suddenly, she felt a sharp pain as vivid memories of the countless events that happened when she turned sixteen flooded her mind. Everyone would say how much she looked like her father; her thick, sandy brown hair was exceptionally long, she thought, as she moved towards the river.

Her skin was smooth and fair, like a light brown paper bag, and her eyes were a hazel color that changed depending on her mood. She was not very tall but an average height for a young lady. She and her mother often talked about her bowed legs and how they resembled her Papa's legs after riding his mule.

Deanna always had a smile to share with anyone she met, but there was no smile on this night. The painful memories were too much. She knew tonight would have to be the night.

As she looked back toward the wooden shack she called home stuffed with all kinds of paper, some from magazines and catalogs to fill the cracks in the walls to keep the heat out in the summer and the cold out in the winter, which now did not make her feel safe, which now seemed like a house of horrors.

She looked back to ensure her brother did not follow her this time. He was sound asleep along with everyone else in the shack. Deanna knew this night had to be the one, no more bearing the pain any longer.

As thoughts continued to race across her mind, painful emotional scars opened and bled a fresh stream of emotional blood. The tears blinded her eyes, and she had to wipe them away to see the path.

The thoughts were now louder than the symphony of the woods. Even the fear of the darkness was silenced by the noise of each heart-wrenching replay. "God," she thought, "if you are real, how could you stand by and allow this to happen? There can't be a God, she said to herself. If so, how? Why? "Thanksgiving is not my favorite holiday anymore."

"Why did momma leave my daddy? This would not be happening if my daddy was around! I know he would believe me," she sighed. More pain, abandonment, and emotional anguish went with her as she moved toward the river.

I was only seven years old, but my daddy loved me. He could be mean sometimes to Momma when he drank moonshine, but I guess Momma got tired of it. I came home from school one day, and she was gone.

This life is too hard. I wish I were a little girl again, visiting with my Big Auntie Emma. I loved going to church, dancing like they do, and when they caught the Spirit. I miss those days of being so innocent and carefree.

My momma had come back and stole me and my sister from Daddy. We moved near my grandfather Papa's house; he was mean, too. He was married to a woman with a heavy, deep voice. When my brother saw her and heard her, he told Momma, "I think Poppa married a man." I could see how my brother thought she was a man. My momma got two sisters and a brother from her, so I am sure she wasn't a man; she laughed.

This is my third time trying to get to the river; I pray it is my last. I don't understand why they don't believe me. God, you know I am telling the truth. I want this over, the pain, the guilt, and the feeling of being alone.

HELP!

Formative Years

It was a scorching summer day, July 14th, 1960, to be exact, in a small town in Louisiana; the nearest hospital was about thirty miles away. This is where I was born. My mother was eighteen when she gave birth to me. According to my mother, Miss Watts, a cousin, took her to the hospital. She also named me Raelynn.

I remember spending most of my childhood living between my mother and Grand-ma-ma. My aunt's youngest daughter also lived with Grand-ma-ma. She was always getting her way. I got furious at her one day, and I patted my butt at her, and she told my Grand-ma-ma, and I got my first and only whooping from her. My Grand-ma-ma said, "You don't pat your butt at nobody, you don't put your tongue out at nobody, and you don't kick anybody."

My mother had gotten married to a good man who treated me like his very own. I remember living in a little house that sat on big brick blocks, that I could crawl under and play with my dog.

One day, I stood in the back of the house looking at the sky. The sun was so bright that it was almost blinding. I was conversing with the sky, and when I was done, there he was. A little white dog, I must have been about three or four. It was something about that little dog; I just loved him.

The dog got a hold of one of the baby chicks we had. As I ran to get it out of his mouth, I ran right into a barbed wire fence, cutting my forehead above my eye. The dog felt terrible for me; he dropped the chick and ran to me. Blood was everywhere as I ran into the house.

My mother washed the cut and placed spider webbing from one of the corners of the house to close the wound. I still have a faint scar to this day.

One day, my mother told me to take two clothespins off the clothesline and then told me to sit on the floor. I thought she was about to comb my hair, but instead, she took two clothes pins and put one on each ear as she began to pierce my ears. She took a sewing needle and burned the tip of it, stuck it through my ears, and left the string in my ears. "Pain." Every day, she would pull the string and put Vaseline and alcohol on my ears until they were ready for earrings. I've never put another piercing in my body.

By the time I turned five, my siblings were born. My mother and her husband lived close to his mother's house. I remember walking through the path of overgrown grass, going to Grandma Ida 's house to play with the other children or get something my mother wanted to borrow. She was a lovely lady with long black hair, very bright skin, almost white, and beautiful bluish-gray eyes. She smiled every time I saw her.

My sister was born in June 1963, and my brother was born in October 1964. He was named after his father, and he looked just like him, too. My sister looked like her grandmother, Miss Ida.

After being at my Grand-ma-ma's and returning to my mother wanting to play in her hair, she had cut it. She tried to look like Diana Ross and the Supremes with the bob in the back and long front sides. I was so upset that all that long, thick hair was gone. I used to stand behind her on the sofa while she sat down and combed her hair. When she took me back to my Grand-ma-ma's house, she wore a scarf and tried to cover up the haircut, but I told my Grand-ma-ma, and she snatched the scarf off and started to whoop her for cutting all that pretty hair.

Grand-ma-ma lived next door to her father, stepmother, two sisters, and brother. Her father, Papa, was tall, dark, and mean-looking. He talked very slowly and sternly. Sometimes, we would all get in his truck to go to town to the local store. I seemed to sit next to him in the truck every time we went somewhere.

They wouldn't let me go on the back with the bigger children. I would try to hold my breath the whole time I was next to him because he was so mean. His denim sleeve had a metal button that would hit the clutch every time he shifted gears. I'll never forget that sound. "Click -"Click "Bing" -"Bing."

Papa's wife, whom we called Motilly, was tall, too. Maybe because I was a child, everybody was tall to me. They went to church all the time.

I loved my Grand-ma-ma's yard. A giant magnolia tree was at the end of the lane on one side, and the school bus tent on the other. She had two big pecan trees, plum trees, fig-trees, and a small field with various vegetables.

When at my Grand-ma-ma's house. I enjoyed sitting on the porch at the end of the day just as the sun went down and the night sound would begin. It was like every creature of the night knew what sounds to make to be in perfect harmony. When it rained, the drops hitting the tin roof were like heaven to me, a calming lullaby that would put me to sleep. However, I didn't like using the out-house at night because it was so dark you couldn't see your hand in front of you or snakes that would crawl inside the out-house.

My Grand-ma-ma had a little farm that supplied her with food. There were chickens, hogs, cows, and a mule for plowing. She also had a big gray cat I didn't like and a dog she called Dog. I loved my Grand-ma-ma's cooking. In the morning, we would wake up to the smell of breakfast OMG, hot biscuits, smoked sausage, grits, eggs, hotcakes, fig jelly, plum jelly, and sugar cane syrup.

One day, my aunt returned from up north to get my cousin, but she cried and said she didn't want to go unless I came too. So, of course, she got her way, and my Grand-ma-ma said you might as well take her too.

I was five years old, and even though I did not want to leave my Grand-ma-ma or see my mother occasionally, I had no say. Children obeyed and went wherever the grown-ups took them, except for my cousin. I said nothing, but inside, I was crying. I felt life was going to be so different for me. It was going to be a whole new world.

We arrived in upstate New York on the train. The ride was long but pleasant. A sharp, cold breeze slapped my face, and chills went through my body as we stepped off the train. It was cold. My aunt pulled two jackets from her big bag and gave them to us to put on. I believe it was on a fall evening. A man was waiting for us.

The man was leaning against a big pink and white car. He was a kind of big man, dark-skinned, with glasses, wearing a suit coat and a brimmed hat, and had a cigar in his mouth. He had pink lips, which were all I had focused on at the time. I didn't know why.

He spoke with a deep voice and opened the front door for my aunt. My cousin pushed me towards the back as the man held the door for us. When the car began moving, my eyes were no longer focused on pink lips. I was looking out the window, noticing how big the buildings were. I was no longer in the country. It felt like I was in a whole new world.

Back home, we would have to walk on the side of the road or through the paths made by others traveling countless times. But when I arrived in Upstate, there were sidewalks everywhere, no dirt roads, more than one stop light, houses were close together, and stores were on street corners.

When the car stopped, we were in front of a green and white house. It was nighttime, and I liked seeing in the dark; this was not so in the country. The man got out and opened my aunt's car door and then ours; we all got out of the car, and my cousin said to my aunt in her slow, long dragging voice, "Mom, I'm hungry." We followed my aunt up the stairs through the side door entrance of the house. The man carried the bags up the stairs into the house.

The house was nice and clean. It had a living room, kitchen, three bedrooms, and a porch upstairs off from the kitchen. Once settled inside, my aunt fixed something for us to eat.

After we ate, she told us to take a bath. The tub was so big both of us could fit in it together. It was not a foot tub like at my Grand-ma-ma's house, where we would have to take turns bathing.

After our bath, we put on our pajamas, entered the bedroom, and got into the bed we had to share. My aunt came to tuck us in. She leaned over, gave my cousin a hug and a kiss, said good night, walked away and turned off the room light—my heart hurt. I could feel sadness well up in me. I wanted to cry. There was no hug or kiss for me! I was crushed. Where is my mother, my Grand-ma-ma? Why am I here?

I silently cried myself to sleep. The following day, the smell of my aunt's biscuits met my nose and woke me up, along with the bright sunlight shining through the bedroom window. My cousin jumped out of bed and ran into the kitchen, and I ran behind her, asking for a buttered biscuit. My aunt turned us around and told us to wash our face and brush our teeth and then showed us how to make our bed; then we had breakfast.

After breakfast, we went outside and sat on the steps, looking at all the people; I only saw white people and little white children playing on the sidewalks and in their yards. There were no Black people anywhere. A little girl yelled from across the street, asking us if we wanted to come and play with her. We told her we could not cross the street. My aunt had told us to stay in the front on the steps.

Someone was working in the little girl's yard, and she asked them if she could cross the street to play with us. When she crossed the street she told us her name was Ruby; she had pretty, brown, wavy long hair and hazel eyes like my mother's. She wasn't as white as most white people, especially those who lived down south. Ruby was very friendly; she had tons of toys and Barbie dolls. She had this toy called a pogo stick that I jumped on every chance I got. We became best friends from that day on.

We also met other children in the neighborhood, Robin, who lived on the corner of our street. There was another girl, I cannot remember her name, who lived around the corner. All I remember about her is that she had ugly warts on her hands. We all played together every chance we got.

At Ruby's house, she had the most games, toys, and a swing set in her yard. It was a fun summer that year.

Ruby talked about school starting soon. My cousin and I were starting the first grade at the neighborhood school. It was within walking distance of where we lived.

I was happy to see Black children in school. My cousin was not in the same classroom as me. I made new friends. A white boy in my class named John sent me a note saying he liked me and thought I was cute. He would always smile and try to sit next to me every chance he'd get. But I had a crush on Myles; he was so cute. He was black, and when he would smile at me, his deep dimples made him much more handsome. He liked me too. Summer had passed so quickly.

Myles asked me on a note if I would be his girlfriend, and I said yes. Every morning, he would bring me a bag of candy, a toy, or a piece of jewelry. Other Black children were in the classroom, and we all became close. We lived near each other and stayed in the same classes throughout the school years.

When it rained, we would put on our bathing suits and play in the puddles, getting our hair wet, which caused it to get nappy and shrink. One day while playing in the rain with Ruby, she asked if she could touch my hair. She seemed amazed at how short it would become.

My other aunt, who lived in the north too, would be the one to hot comb our hair and fuss the whole time she did it about playing in the rain. She would turn the oven on, and we would lean our heads in the oven until our hair dried. Then, she would hot comb it out, burn me, and tell me it was the grease. I knew it was her talking, not paying attention, and not the grease. I must admit that my hair looked nice when she finished. Ruby did not know about the process for us to get straight hair.

The years went by very quickly at the red brick building. My first school fight was in the fifth grade. Myles and I had been together as girlfriend and boyfriend since the second grade, and everyone knew it except for the new girl, Debra, who started attending at the end of that year. Her long hair made her attractive. Rumors spread throughout the school that she wanted to fight me because she liked Myles.

Little did I know she was waiting for me in front of the school building on the Friday before the last week of school. I was a safety guard assigned to a particular door, and Myles would always wait with me until I finished my post. Earlier that day, Gwen, one of the tough girls, gave me a big ring to wear. Someone came to where I was standing and told me that Debra was waiting for me at the end of the walkway, with a crowd of my so-called friends standing on her side, my cousin included.

I strolled down the sidewalk to the end of the fence and the opening, where they all stood. Debra stopped me as I continued walking as if I did not know what was happening. Myles and I were on one side, and Debra and the entire school were on the other side. She said, "I'm going to kick your butt." The crowd said, "Get her." Then Debra raised her arm as if to hit me; I grabbed her collar and held it as I used the other hand with the ring on it to punch her in the eye.

As blood began to gush from her face, the chants from the crowd changed to "Get her, Raelynn," including my cousin. I never started any fights, but for whatever reason, girls, primarily dark-skinned ones, did not like me. Of course, I got in big trouble that day. I didn't know until later that Debra and her sisters had come to my house. She had a big patch on her eye. They said I almost put her eye out. Years later, I saw her, and she still has the scar.

I told my side of the story, and my uncle, who picked us up from the train station, said it looked like she did not win that fight. He told them to take it as that and leave it alone. They were upset, but they left.

The school year was over for the summer, and we were all so excited to be going to the sixth grade next year and Summer Soul School, a day camp. Where we did arts and crafts, camping, dancing, and putting on live talent shows. That was when I got my period, something I knew nothing about. That day, I wore white shorts to camp and did not feel a thing except for what I thought was sweat from the heat.

One of the boys yelled, "You got blood on your shorts. I thought I had sat in something until I went to the bathroom to look in the mirror, and my panties were wet with blood. I put tissue in my panties because the blood was still coming. One of the girls gave me her sweater to put around my waist. I left camp right then and walked home.

After bathing, I changed my clothes and hid the bloody shorts and underwear behind the washing machine. My aunt found them and asked us whose they were. Of course, my cousin snitched. The boy at the camp told her what happened because I had left her there. We were supposed to walk home together.

My aunt told me we do not hide or throw clothes away; we wash them before putting them into the laundry. I was beyond embarrassed. My older cousin Lee told me a little more about my period because she was already getting hers. I would not say I liked it, but I had to live with it.

I could not help thinking, why didn't someone tell me about this? Where was my mother? Shouldn't a mother tell you about these things? I was ashamed and surprised. What does all this mean? Am I going to bleed forever? When will it stop? There was no answer to the questions in my mind, only a Kotex strap and big, thick pads. I felt like I had a baby's diaper on.

We had moved across the bridge to Bartlett Street, where other Black people lived, the neighborhood was nice. I was turning twelve that July, and my aunt gave me a birthday party. I think she was trying to make me feel better in her own way.

Myles and I were no longer together as girlfriend and boyfriend after I found out he was the one who had told Debra's sisters where I lived. So, a cute boy named Andrew, who lived around the block, came with his brother Cedrick to my party. My cousin and I were in the Sunshine Band at church, a youth choir. The children from the choir also came to the party.

I liked attending church; my aunt would ensure we were dressed nicely. Everything matched our shoes, purses that matched our hats, or bows in our hair. You did not leave the house looking any kind of way. My aunt made sure of that. Sometimes, she would dress me and my cousin alike. I hated that, even at my birthday party, we had the same thing on but different colors.

My party was dope. We were outside while the older people were in the house, laughing and talking about God knows what. I had never had a birthday party before. Sometimes, when my birthday came, I would forget it was my birthday, having been bounced around from place to place.

I was twelve and wondered why my mother did not want me. I wrote her a letter after my cousin Butch cut my finger while playing with a straight razor, and I had to get seven stitches. One day before that happened, he smashed my head in the top part of the refrigerator. He didn't seem to get in trouble for anything. I just felt so alone in a house full of people who were darker skinned tone than me, and they teased me often about it.

Well, the letter I wrote to my mother returned, and my aunt opened it and read it. I did not know you could not reuse mailing stamps. I had put things in the letter about what I was going through and how I was being treated. My aunt sent me back down south to my Grand-ma-ma's. I did not find out until later that it was because of the letter I sent with a used stamp.

By this time, my mother had separated from her husband and moved to the house opposite my Grand-ma-ma's. I had to babysit my younger sisters and brothers when my mother would go out to work. I was happy to be with my Grand-ma-ma but did not know my siblings. I only knew them as little people I had to look out for.

When I went to church with my Grand-ma-ma, one lady there asked me if I had seen my father. I thought, my father, why would she ask me that? A man stopped by to see me some time, but I did not know who he was. I thought that was who she could be talking about; I just said no. So, I asked my Grand-ma-ma if I could see my father, who this lady was talking about. She told me where he lived, and I looked him up in the phone book and called him. He answered the phone. When I asked for him, he immediately knew who I was, and he asked how I was doing and how long I would be down here. I answered his question and then asked if I could see him. There was a moment of silence on the other end of the phone, and then he said I will try to see you before you go.

A day later, this very tall, handsome, clean-cut man knocked on my Grand-ma-ma's house door. I opened the door to let him in. I just looked at him to see if I looked like him. I looked at every part of him: his eyes, his nose, his ears, his hands, even his body shape. Then he smiled, and all I saw was gold; he had all these gold teeth.

He reached to hug me, and I reached back. I thought, if this was my father, I would want a hug, and I didn't want him ever to let me go. My father, my very own daddy, everyone has a daddy, I thought, but me. Even my sisters and brothers' fathers would pick them up after he and my mom separated; now, my father is coming to see me.

The Relationship

He asked me how I was doing up north; I just smiled and said OK. He asked me if I needed anything. I wanted to say yes, I need you, but I knew I would not get him even if I asked for him. My mind flooded with questions.

Why am I now twelve, and I am not with you? Why do you have to come here to see me? Why am I not with you and the other children you have? Why don't you want me either? I just said, "No, I don't need anything." As he stood up to go, he gave me another hug. I wanted to go with him so the hugs would never stop.

I went to church that Sunday, and he was in the choir there. I was so happy to see him again. After church, he spoke to me but was a little distant when his wife came up beside him with two children. He introduced them to me; they were very standoffish. I thought, here we go again, not knowing why I felt rejected.

After church, when we reached home, The phone was ringing as we walked in, and Grand-ma-ma answered it; as I headed to the bathroom, I could hear the person on the phone with my Grand-ma-ma say, "Every time she comes down there that woman has something to say. It is always a mess. Raelynn might as well come back up here." I thought I was returning to the cold, and my cousins were back up north. Wow! I don't even know what I did. It didn't matter; I knew I would not be here long. I'm sure I won't be back down here again anytime soon.

What is it?

Now that I have returned north, I'm living with my Auntie Em and enjoying it. She worked at a local grocery store and always brought home all kinds of good food. Auntie Em was beautiful to me. She had bright skin and almost looked like a white woman with nice black hair. She was of average build and had skinny legs.

Auntie Em always went to bingo. I would be home alone a lot when I lived with her. I would love to clean her room because I always find her loose change. She made me stop cleaning it because she could never find anything once I did, and she realized she wasn't seeing any of her loose change around. She would use it at bingo when she did not have bingo chips.

While living with Auntie Em, I started Junior High at West High School on Genesee Street. I liked going to school until this big girl wanted to fight me for no reason. I would run home every day until I got tired of running. Well, that was the day we fought.

It was on one of those chilly winter days after a snowfall in front of the school. She came up behind me and pushed me down. She said I did something to her cousin Jackie. Jackie was a girl in one of my classes. I had thought her folder was mine and had mistakenly wrote on it. I told her I was sorry, but I knew she did not like me because of how she looked at me, and I didn't dress that well, not like I did when I was with my other aunt.

Jackie always looked nice and neatly combed hair. I would do my hair in a ponytail or mushroom style, which was what I wore most days. When the big girl pushed me, I fell on my face in the snow. Then she pulled me up, but I managed to pull away and grab her coat, and she landed on top of me. I just started biting her in her chest. She tried to tear away, but I kept chewing until one of the school sentries broke us up.

She was holding her chest where I had bitten her. I could see the blood on her blouse. I told the sentry she started the fight, but I would end it. Everyone who saw the fight reported the same story: I had no bruises, just wet from the wet, cold, slushy snow. I was freezing on the walk home.

I was glad Auntie Em did not get home before me. She would be mad because my hair got wet, and she had just pressed it the night before. I'll braid it so she can't see it. She noticed everything, even if she didn't say anything about it. She made sure I was clean not going to bed with dirty feet.

While living with her, I fell asleep on the sofa one night and woke up to it being on fire. I don't know how it started, but I was blamed for it. Auntie Em thought I was trying to smoke and left a lit cigarette on the edge of the sofa. I never tried to smoke and didn't like the smell of smoke, nor did I like to be around when she was smoking.

I was sent back to Aunt V's because of the fire. Counting my many moves, I started with Aunt V, then Uncle Beard and Auntie May, back south with my Grand-ma-ma, and back north with Aunt V. In one of those moves back to Aunt V's, I met Joy. She was one of my cousin's girlfriends who hung out with my Auntie Em.

Every time Joy came over, she would ask about me, what I was doing, and where I was. She seemed to be the only one who cared about me. Don't get me wrong, they all cared, but Joy was more attentive to me; she wanted to know what was happening with me. She would ask Aunt V if I could go with her to different places. I remember when she got her first apartment, and I had Chinese food for dinner for the first time there. Joy made me feel special.

Joy taught me a lot; I remember her teaching me how to ride the city bus. At that moment, I recognized that I learned something new from each person I lived with. I learned to play cards, especially when Casino Bill and his wife came up from the South to live with Uncle Beard.

My aunt and uncle would host club meetings. I liked those because they would have all kinds of gourmet food, drinks, and sweets. The music was loud. The children had to remain in their rooms and could only come out when they wanted us to entertain them with dancing. My mother must have danced her whole pregnancy with me because I love to dance.

All the music of the '50s, '60s, and '70s was my favorite. I pretended that Diana Ross was my mother, and I was going to marry Michael Jackson and cheat on him with Jackie. My cousins found it strange that I liked Elvis Presley and his movies. I could imitate him and sing some of his songs. I sometimes wished I had grown up in those times.

My Aunt V had bought her house, so the club meetings were now hosted at her spot. The house was big; it had a living room, dining room, and enclosed porch off from the living room. I liked the nice-sized kitchen with the pantry and window facing the backyard. There was a side door that led into the kitchen and the basement. The upstairs had four bedrooms; one of the bedrooms had a back porch. I thought that was cool; in the summer, when it was hot, my cousin and I would sleep out there sometime.

I'm back living with my cousins Ann, Lee, and their brother Butch again. My aunt had five children, but those three were the only ones living there. I was still able to go to the same junior high school. Lee was about four years older than me. She was a cheerleader at her school, and she and her friends would teach Ann and me some of their cheers. Ann couldn't dance. Lee could dance well when we entertained at the club meetings. She always wanted to play Gladys Knight and the Pips. She was Gladys, and we were the Pips minus one.

Butch (the one who cut me playing with a razor) walked around like he was god's gift to the world. He was funny and made us laugh all the time, telling jokes. Butch would be the preacher when we acted like the people in our church. We had lots of fun most of the time when my aunt wasn't home.

Butch would tease me by calling me a yellow submarine. Not because I was big or anything, it was because they all were dark-skinned. He would sing his version of the song by the Beatles, "We All Live with the Yellow Submarine." Lee and Ann would join in. "I hate that song to this day."

Aunt V's boyfriend, now husband, who I called Uncle D, the same man who picked us up from the train station; he never said my name right, and he called me shit color. Shit was his favorite word; some of his sentences would start with shit. I liked him despite all that. He was a hard-working man, and he made sure our bellies were full when we would go out to eat.

He was a deacon in our church and would grill us after each service, asking us what the preacher talked about and what was his topic. Where did he take his text from? It was his way of knowing if we were paying attention in church.

Then he would tell me not to believe everything those devilish preachers tell me. I thought, "Listen to the preacher, but don't believe everything he says." Uncle D was a Baptist Deacon and took it seriously. We couldn't do anything on Sunday but go to church, come home, and have dinner, which was my favorite thing on Sundays.

The other thing we could do on Sunday was clean the kitchen; my aunt did not believe in using paper plates. She used China, and the table was always set. When I say clean the kitchen, it wasn't just washing the dishes; it was putting the leftovers away, washing the dishes, sweeping the floor, wiping the counters, and, if needed, mopping the floor. She would always want the kitchen cleaned after dinner (all the rooms had better be clean). She would say you don't know what could happen in the night; you don't want people coming in and seeing a messy house.

I'm grateful to her for that lesson. Although I didn't like it then, it was one of many things she taught that helped make me the woman I am today.

One afternoon, when I came home from school, my aunt called me to her room and handed me an envelope that she had already opened: a Christmas card with money. She said it was from my father. It was close to Christmas. I thanked her and walked out of the room, happy and confused.

I was happy to get the card but confused about why he didn't want me. The thought was short-lived because my aunt yelled from the room for me to clean the bathroom. I loved the new house, and we cleaned all the time. It was spotless. While cleaning the bathroom, I stopped and looked at myself in the mirror. My body was changing, and it was outgrowing my mind.

My face was full of pimples; my breasts were growing so big I wondered when they would stop; hair was in places I never knew it was to be. I couldn't hide what was going on with my body; it just kept changing. I wish someone would have warned me about all of this. The boys stared at me all the time. I wanted to hide. I didn't like them starring. There was nothing I could do. It was happening without my permission.

Christmas had come and gone; spring was in the air. Ann asked if I would go with her to the local library down the street from the house. On the way there, she told me that she was going to meet a boy named Teddy and his brother. Teddy was one of her classmates. His brother's name was Lamont.

When we got home, Aunt V called me to her room. She told me my mother, sisters, and brothers were moving here. She said I could continue to stay with her or go and live with my mother. She said I didn't have to give her an answer now but when my mother got here. I left her room, went and sat on the floor in our room, and thought, wow, I get to decide for myself now; I get to say where I want to live.

Did I want to live with someone I didn't know, and I hated for letting me go and not wanting me? Did she even want me to live with her now? This was all too much. Why couldn't my aunt say your mother is moving here and you will stay with her? Why do I have to choose?

On the other hand, I could be with my real sisters and brothers. Maybe it will be a real family. I will have a little freedom because Aunt V is strict. There was too much for me to think about, my thoughts were interrupted by the smell of the food cooking downstairs. I went downstairs to the kitchen, and on the stove was one of my favorite meals: red beans and rice, fried barbeque chicken, homemade hot buttered cornbread fresh out of the oven. As I ate, I thought it would be hard to leave. One thing I would genuinely miss is Aunt V's cooking.

The phone rang just as we finished cleaning the dinner dishes. To my surprise, it was Lamont. I was happy that Ann answered it; if my aunt had answered, I would have had a lot of explaining and would not have been able to talk to him.

He said I called to see if you gave me the correct phone number. If I didn't want you to have my number, I wouldn't have given it to you and said no, you can't have it. That would be like lying, right; me giving you the wrong number. He said, "So you are a goody two shoe. No, I replied. I like being honest because when you lie, you forget the lies and get caught up in them anyway. So, I try not to practice lying.

Then he asked how old I was. I told him in a couple of months, I would be 13. He laughed and said I was lying because I looked older than thirteen. I could see why he would think that all he looked at was a big balloon-looking breast. I told him I was not and hoped you didn't think I wanted a boyfriend. Anyway, how old are you? He said he was seventeen. I heard Aunt V walking upstairs, told him I had to go, and hung up the phone quickly.

When I saw Teddy in school, he didn't say hi, hello, or anything. He asked, "Why did you hang up on my brother?" I told him, I said goodbye and that I had to go. Isn't that what people do when they are done talking? So, I hung up. How old is your brother anyway? He replied seventeen. I don't know why I even cared about his age; It wasn't like we would be boyfriend and girlfriend.

Lamont and I talked on the phone a lot. I shared with him about the decision I had to make to stay with my aunt or stay with my mother. He said he wouldn't tell me what to do; the choice was mine, and "didn't you want to be with your family"?

All I could think was she gave me away; she didn't want me; why should I live with someone who didn't want me? I will think about what you said. I ended the conversation because I was feeling the need to be alone. I wanted to cry and suck my thumb. My thumb was my comfort, my security, and my food was my comfort, too.

So many people tried everything in the book to stop me from sucking my thumb. My aunt went as far as getting a worm and putting it in my room on the dresser and said if she caught me with my thumb in my mouth that she would wrap the worm around my thumb and make me suck it then. She knew I was afraid of worms.

One night, I tried to drown the worm by putting water in the cup. It didn't work. Then I poured mouthwash into the cup, and the worm swarmed around and died. I poured the mouthwash out before my aunt could see it. Later in the week, my aunt found the worm dead in the cup, and she never caught me with my thumb in my mouth.

The day of the decision came; I chose to move in with my mother. I called her by her first name, not mom, mommy, or mother. I didn't know how to give her respect or how to honor her as my mother. She had gotten an apartment in the same building as my cousin Biscuit and his wife. They lived next door. Cousin Biscuit was my aunt's oldest son.

He was always on governmental vacations for long periods of time.

His wife had a daughter when they got married, and later they had one together. The apartment was okay; I wasn't used to living in apartments because everywhere I lived at was a house, even if it was double-sided. I liked that my room had a fire escape at the window I sat on at night when it was hot.

My siblings were younger than me. My three sisters were Stacie, ten, nicknamed Stai; Dynetta, seven, nicknamed Dee; and Yolanda, five, nicknamed Bobbie, after my mom's brother, who died when she was pregnant with her. She and he were very close. She did that to honor him: my two brothers, Little J, nine, and Terrell, who was eight.

I became more like their mother; my mother worked and stayed gone most of the time. We were pretty much on our own. There was no more going to church, no more Sunday rules, and, most of all, no more big Sunday dinners. What a big difference.

Lamont and I still talked on the phone. He knew I had decided to stay with my mother. I told him he could come and meet them one day if he wanted to. The day he came over, he laughed and joked with them about how country they were. He said they talk real Geechee. My sister Stai said, "I ain't no Gucci." We cracked up laughing because she sounded like a Geechee.

They liked Lamont. He dropped out of school at sixteen. I would babysit for my cousin next door and give him money to catch the bus to different places looking for a job. Once Lamont got a job and was paid, he would buy things we needed, like clothes, shoes, and food. My mother was nothing like my aunt when it came to dressing us, preparing good meals, or keeping a clean house. The house seemed never to stay clean. I had to make them clean behind themselves, do the girls' hair, and make sure they all took baths. Whenever they wanted or needed anything, they would come to me.

I told Lamont everything. I needed someone to talk to, and he needed a friend. He would tell me about his girlfriend, how she didn't take good care of herself, and her hygiene. He said she always smelled. He would come over just to get away from home when his mother would be drinking and get drunk. He said she would hit them with anything when she was intoxicated, and please don't let her cook. He said the food would be too salty or have too much black pepper, and he couldn't eat it.

Lamont had five brothers and one sister, Teddy being the youngest. Lamont and I became very close friends and were able to share. He treated my brothers and sisters as if they were his very own blood.

One day, I was babysitting for my cousin, and Lamont came over. My mother was home next door, and one of my siblings told her he was there with me. She came over and told me I needed to go and do the dishes; I said OK. I guess I wasn't moving fast enough for her. I was telling Lamont he had to go and say my goodbyes before I was finished; she came back over with a belt and started to whoop me in front of Lamont. Yelling and screaming, "Didn't I tell you to come and wash the dishes?"

I felt something inside of me snap. Lamont left, and as I walked into our kitchen, she was still whooping me. When I got to the sink of dishes, I filled a glass with hot water, turned around to her, held the glass up, and told her if she hit me one more time, I was going to throw the glass of water in her face.

She stopped, looked at me, and said boys are nasty, and you don't need to be around them. I was so angry that I felt the blood boil and go to my head. I wanted to kill her at that moment. I had never felt that before; I didn't know such rage could be in me. Maybe it was all my hatred for her coming to the surface. I was never the same after that day.

I overheard my Aunt Em and cousin's wife talking about me just as I was about to knock on the door. My aunt said I know she is having sex because her hips are getting wide; she has a boyfriend. I didn't have a boyfriend, and I wasn't all that educated on the sex thing either. They talk too much about what they don't know.

Lamont would tell me about him and his girlfriend having sex and how she smelled most of the time. I told him I didn't want to do that until I was grown and married. I am too young for that anyway. It didn't help that my body was so developed that I couldn't hide it. Lamont had become a part of my reality, as well as being with my sisters and brothers. Despite all the things I missed being at Aunt V's, I was with my own family. I had come to trust Lamont, and he confided in me.

He called one day and told me that he and his girlfriend had gotten into a fight, and her family jumped on him because he hit her. They broke up. I told him I don't blame her for breaking up with you. I wish my cousin's wife would break up with him because he hit her, too.

I told him you shouldn't hit a girl. When I would see and hear some of the things that caused my cousin to hit his wife, I said to myself I would never ask my husband about other women, and if he loves me and marries me, we won't have that problem, he will only want to be with me. Lamont said she got smart-mouthed with him, which made him angry, so he hit her. I said no excuse and hung up.

It was Memorial Day weekend, and my cousin's wife asked me to babysit for her. She, Joy, and Auntie Em were going out with two other friends. I babysat at her house, next door. I had put the girls to bed. While listening to the music, the phone rang. It was Lamont; he had my cousin's phone number and knew I was babysitting that night. We talked about the music and the songs that were playing on the radio; we were listening to the same station.

He liked it when a song came on; he would try to sing along, and when my favorite song came on, I would do the same and dance, holding the phone. Break Up to Make Up came on, and he asked if I would be his girlfriend because he was not making up with his girlfriend.

I said not now; I am too young, and I know you and your girlfriend were having sex, and I am not going to be having sex with you. I want to be married. He said he would wait until I got done with school. I said OK.

I thought about how I could confide in him and how much my siblings loved him, and he loved them. He asked if he could come over and see me. I told him for a little while because it was getting late. We hung up. I went to look in the mirror to see if I looked ok. Why did I care now?

I didn't care how he saw me before. Before he was Lamont, my confidant and friend, I wondered why I was now concerned. Lamont got there so fast; I was still in the bathroom looking in the mirror when he knocked on the door.

Show and Tell

When he came in, the radio was still on the same station. As he sat on the sofa, I offered him a glass of Kool-Aid; my cousin made the best Kool-Aid. I got us both a glass and sat at the other end of the sofa. He asked, "Why are you sitting so far away?" Something was different. He even looked different. Is this what it is like to go from being a confidant and friend to being together as a girlfriend and boyfriend?

This was nothing like me and Myles in grammar school. This was different. Lamont asked if he could kiss me, and I said OK. When he kissed me, he put his tongue in my mouth. I pushed him away and said that is so nasty. He said it is called a French kiss. I told him that French kisses are nasty. He said he would teach me how to do it. I became a student of French kissing.

We kissed again about the third time. I felt a strange sensation, weird but good. I could feel the nipples on my breast get erect and a heat rising from my box, as my Grand-ma-ma would call it. Lamont pulled me closer to him. I could see his pants bulge at the zipper. I felt his penis as our bodies touched. The song playing on the radio was Show and Tell.

He said he didn't believe I was a virgin and that I was going to have to show and tell tonight. I pushed him away and told him he had to go; he kept saying "I had to show and tell." I got up, went to the door, and told him he had to leave my house, saying, "I don't need to prove anything to you."

I had to use the bathroom; I felt like I was going to pee on myself. I told him to go and ran to the bathroom. My panties were wet; I know I didn't pee on myself. I didn't know what was going on with my body. I had never felt like this before. I felt dirty, so I decided to take a bath. While I ran the bath water, I went downstairs to ensure Lamont was gone and locked the door.

He was gone, but the door was not locked. So, I locked it and turned off the radio. I went back upstairs, got one of my cousin's wife's nightgowns, took my bath, looked in on the girls, who were sound asleep, and got into bed in the spare bedroom.

I couldn't help but think about what just happened. Lord, I don't think I should see Lamont anymore. I don't think he is going to wait. As that prayer crossed my mind, I heard a noise in the closet. I got scared; I thought it was mice until I saw the door open, and Lamont came out. Oh my God, what are you doing here?

He got on the bed and said, "You are going to show and tell tonight." I wanted to scream and yell, but I didn't want to wake the girls or my mother next door. I just said, "Lamont, I am a virgin, and I don't want to do this."
He pulled his pants off, put his hand over my mouth, and said, "I don't believe you; you kiss too well." I knew he wasn't going to let me go.

I started to cry; I became very numb as I lay there like a dead person. He took his hand off my mouth and tried to kiss me. I just turned my head and begged him to stop. I said no, I didn't want to do this. He pulled my gown up and touched my box and tried to push his penis inside of me.

The more he pushed, the more painful it was. I kept repeating to him to stop, and it hurt. I don't want to do this. He just said it would feel better once he got in. I knew I was at the point of no return, and he did not care about my feelings. I just died a little more inside. When he was done, he fell over onto the bed and said, "I'm sorry you were a virgin."

I just hurt and cried. I asked, "Would you please leave?" he just continued to say how sorry he was. You're sorry won't give me back what you just took. Please leave! He finally left when I said my cousin would be home soon.

I'm going to have to be his girlfriend forever now. Lord, I wanted my husband to do that. I want to die. I felt so wet I went to the bathroom and blood was everywhere. I even had to change the sheets on the bed. I threw the bloody sheets away. I wish I could have thrown that night away like those sheets.

I couldn't change anything about that night; one thing for sure, I would never be a virgin again. Lord, this is not what I wanted. It hurt so badly, my body and my soul. It wasn't supposed to be like this. I feel so dirty. My mother was right, boys are nasty. I took another bath. The bleeding wouldn't stop. The bath water was bloody. I found a Kotex pad under the cabinet and put it on.

What am I to do now?

The next day, my cousin found the sheets in the trash. I told her my period came on and messed them up. I thought, "I know I should have washed them out as Aunt V taught me, but I didn't want any reminders of last night." She left them in the trash.

Lamont called me later that day, but I wouldn't talk to him. I didn't speak to him for weeks. One day, there was a knock at the door. I would never have opened the door if I knew it was Lamont on the other side. When he saw me, he fell on his knees and begged me to forgive him.

I was still hurting more emotionally than physically. How can I forgive you for taking something you can't give back, nor can I get it back? I asked him to leave, but my little sister saw him at the door and pulled him in. They had not seen him for weeks. I was no longer comfortable around him. Our friendship had changed.

He stayed talking to my sister and brother, giving them money to go to the corner store so he could speak to me alone. He said I am sorry again. I told him to stop apologizing because sorry could not change anything that happened. I told him I didn't want to see him anymore and I didn't want to be his girlfriend.

He said I want you to know I've been sick, throwing up and stuff. I think you are pregnant. I think you got that all wrong. The girl gets sick; at least, that's what they said in health class. How do you get the sickness, and I'm pregnant? I asked him to leave before my sisters and brothers returned from the store. As he left, he repeated it: I'm so sorry. I didn't mean to hurt you. I pushed him out the door and said, 'bye, Lamont'.

Two weeks had gone by since I saw Lamont, and I was late for my period. Oh, my God, could it be true, God, please? I can't be pregnant; I'm too young for this; please don't let it be true, God. I would pray and cry and pray and cry.

I finally went to the teen clinic and had a test done. When they came in the room and told me that I was and my due date was January, I wanted to roll up in a ball and die.

I never wanted to see Lamont again, but now I will have to tell him and be his girlfriend because I don't want to have anyone else raise my baby, and I want him to have what I didn't: a mother and a father.

When I got home, I called Lamont and told him. He responded, "I knew it because I had been so sick, and my mother told me, "Boy, you just got one of those nappy-headed girls pregnant." Then he said I will marry you as soon as you get out of school. I promise. I felt like I had no choice at this point. My God, how am I going to tell my mother? Well, Lamont took care of that. He wrote her a letter without my knowing.

When she got the letter and found out, my Aunt Em and my cousin's girlfriend discussed me as if I wasn't there or a part of the issue. My cousin said I was too young and should have an abortion. My aunt and mother said no, she made her bed, and she would lay in it. I would have killed myself with my baby inside of me before I had an abortion. All I could think about was, "I have someone inside me, and I will always love them, and they love me, and their mine.

My mother and I didn't get along; I'm sure it didn't help that she and I had a fistfight about a month before all of this happened. The police were called. She wanted to put me away. I had gotten drunk with my cousin Bern and his friend. They asked my mother before I drank if it was okay. It was Colt, 45 tall boys. They bet me if I could drink two of them straight.

My mother told them beer was good for children and kills worms. When she said that I took the first can down, it went so fast; the second and half of a third of the time, they couldn't believe it. It was my first time drinking. I was sitting down, and when I stood up to go to the bathroom, a mad rush went to my head as I wobbled to the stairs, still holding the third can of Colt 45.

My little sister Bobbie, who talked too much except when watching her favorite TV show, started chanting "Nah" Nah," Raelynn drunk. I didn't think about it; I just shot the beer can down the stairs, and it hit her on the head; she went screaming, and my mother started yelling. I slid down the stairs, and she started hitting me. I remember jumping around like a boxer would in a boxing ring and telling her to come on let's fight.

I didn't remember if she hit me. But I remember I was in the big-armed chair when the police came and asked what the problem was. I just burst out, "I'm just drunk, and I hit my sister in the head with a can of beer because she wouldn't be quiet. And then my mother said, "Take her," but the police must have told her to let me sleep it off because the next thing I remembered was waking up the next day and the new outfit that Lamont had bought me was ripped and hanging off me and my arms all bruised up.

Now that I was pregnant, my mom and I weren't getting along, so I moved in with my cousin Biscuit's wife. She finally left him and moved out of the apartment.

I was not allowed to go to public school. I had to go to the Young Mother's Program at the YWCA; they helped me to continue my education and with any assistance that was available to young mothers. I didn't mind going because there were other young girls pregnant like me.

Lamont was still a part of my life, and he was supportive but had become very jealous and possessive. He would get agitated if I spoke to another boy I may have known from school or the past. He wouldn't say anything until we were alone, and then he would say stuff like wait until we got by ourselves. Then he would slap me or punch me and tell me to jump bitch if you think you're bad.

I didn't do anything but cry when he left, and I would say to myself, "God gonna get you." I remembered a bible verse from Sunday school when I went to church with my aunt, which said, "Vengeance is mine, said the Lord, and I shall repay."

By this time, Lamont and I were spending a lot of time together, and he still wanted me to have sex with him. I hated it. He would force me all the time. I would just lay there and think, I don't want to be like my mother and my Aunt V, having children by more than one man. I want to keep my son with a mother and a father. So, I'll have to take what I get.

Sex was still so painful. One day, Lamont took me to his brother & his wife's house, and while we were sitting and talking, one of his brother's friends pulled out a brown envelope, poured out this dried grass-looking stuff, and began to put it in some thin white paper, and rolled it up like a cigarette. He lit it and began to smoke it; it smelled so bad. He took about two puffs, held the smoke in, blew it out, and passed it to Lamont's brother.

The friend then rolled another one and passed it to Lamont. Lamont lit it, took two or three puffs, then passed it to me and told me to draw the smoke in and hold it for a few minutes, then let it out. I did, and I instantly felt a rush, something I had never felt before.

It felt good. I felt a calm come over every part of my being. This is crazy, but I liked it. It was reefer, weed, pot. I didn't care what they called it; it made me feel good. I was high for the first time. I was so hungry and thirsty. I could feel my highness coming down. Lamont's sister-in-law gave me some Kool-Aid. She had a grape flavor. It was so good, but my throat was so dry. I'm sure it was from the weed.

We sat around smoking more and listening to Isaac Hayes and New Birth. I felt like dancing, but I didn't. It was my first time meeting them, and I didn't feel comfortable dancing in front of them, much less Lamont. I don't think I had ever danced in front of him or with him as much as I loved to do it.

When we left there, I was so high that I couldn't stop smiling or laughing. My eyes felt dry and heavy. I still like what I was feeling. No one was home when we got there; Lamont started kissing me and feeling all over my breast; it felt different now that I was high. I began to kiss back, and he took my hand and put it on his penis. It was hard. I was scared for some reason.

I felt like this was not right, so I pulled my hand away, but he put it back and said just hold it. As he continued to caress my breast and feel other parts of my body, I started to feel good. I'm sure it was because I was high. I wanted to tell him to stop because I knew it was going to hurt if we had sex. My mind was thinking one thing, but my body was beginning to do its own thing.

We went from standing in my room to lying on the bed. Just as he was about to pull my pants down, the doorbell rang. We rushed and put our clothes back on. I ran downstairs to the door. It was my cousin's daughter, and she had forgotten her key. Lamont was still upstairs using the bathroom. She looked hard at me and asked if I was crying because my eyes were so red from being high. I told her no; I was just tired. Then she said my clothes smelled funny. I smelled like weed and didn't know it.

Lamont came downstairs and said he was about to go. I was so glad he was. He said he would call me later. We became boyfriend and girlfriend, which I did not want because I was so young. But I was carrying our baby, which made him very possessive of me. I couldn't talk to boys or schoolmates. He wanted to know everywhere I went. And I better not get smart-mouthed with him.

I did one time and had to wear makeup to school to cover the bruises from a black eye and a busted lip. So, I would get smart-mouthed under my breath. I didn't tell anybody that Lamont was hitting me. I was afraid to because I didn't know what would happen to him. I still cared for him as a friend. Plus, I wanted my baby to have his father in his life.

While living with my cousin during my pregnancy, I was playing around in the playground with one of my young cousins, and my water broke. I thought I was peeing on myself and couldn't control it. It was early; I was only seven months along. When I got to the hospital, they said I would have to stay because the baby's lungs would not be developed enough, and they didn't want me to get an infection because the baby sack was broken. Lamont came every day to be with me, and my mother and my cousin Lee came too.

It was getting close to Thanksgiving, and I had been in the hospital for almost two weeks now. On November 22nd, I started to have some pain, like my period when it would come on. My cousin was visiting me, and we were laughing and joking around, but the pain started to get worse. I wasn't laughing anymore. My cousin left, and Lamont returned because he had gone for a while.

I was in labor. My baby was about to be born, or so I thought. One whole day went by, and a night, they didn't give me anything for the pain. I just moaned and tried not to cry. I prayed. I said to God, if I ever do this again, I will be married and know the man loves me, never again. Shifts came and went, some good nurses and some mean ones. It was probably because I was so young, and they wanted me to feel every pain; little did they know I was living in pain, but this pain was altogether different.

The night shift nurse was a short, old white lady whose white shoes looked turned up at the toes. She would come and check on me from time to time. Lamont was sitting in the chair next to the bed. It was about midnight when the doctor came and checked on me and said I wasn't ready;

Around 1 a.m., I could feel the baby coming, and I yelled, "It's coming." Lamont woke up, and the nurse, with her mean self and turned-up white shoes, came in, gapped my legs open, looked, and said, "Yep, yep, there it is."

The doctor came in and said it was time to push. I gave about two pushes, and this little screaming baby came out. They announced it was a boy born 11/24 at 1:40 am, 2 lbs. 11 oz. I thought he was only two pounds, all that pain, and he was only two pounds. Then I thought my love is here. I felt a love I couldn't explain, and all the pain was worth it.

Because he was so tiny, he had to be in the NIC Unit. His lungs weren't fully developed, and he needed to gain weight. The next day, my mother, sisters, and brothers came to see our baby. They all had a gift in their hands, and it made me feel good to see them and to see my mother with a smile on her face as she looked at her grandson. She seemed proud.

Wow, I was 14 and a mother. I felt happy and shameful at the same time. I was happy to have a love of my own and ashamed because I was so young, and I wondered what people would think of me.

Most of me didn't care because I now had someone who would always be there and love me. He is also my teach me, baby. He has taught me never to have another baby until I am married and know the man loves me. I promised myself that while in labor, never again until that time.

Lamont was happy to have a son. He named him after himself, a junior; he had my last name because we weren't married. He was a good father under the circumstances, him being 18 and not finishing school. He did have a job. He made sure I had milk and diapers.

Lamont made me feel like he owned me, and I didn't want to be with anyone else because he was my son's father, and he had taken something from me that I only wanted the man I would marry to have. What was I to do?

I did like it when we smoked weed together. He would make sure we had food for when we got the munchies. However, I didn't like him pushing me to have sex. I hated it; it was so painful, both physically and emotionally. I would lie sometimes, telling him my period was on, but he didn't care. We would fight; well, he would do the hitting. I still wouldn't have sex because he would know I lied.

I moved with my mother when school started that fall. I was on the other side of town from Lamont. He would still come and see me and Lamont Jr., who I nick-named Junior.

I'll Be There

We had a big fight, and I was tired, so I told him I couldn't take it anymore. I told him I was too young to be going to school trying to hide bruises. And not to mention, one of my cousins wanted to give me a gun and told me to kill you the next time you hit me. I broke up with Lamont. I was so sad and depressed.

I had a newfound freedom that I didn't understand. I was living in a new place and going to a new school. I was back with my siblings again, feeling like I was their mom. My mother was one of the first to move into these new apartments on the east side, a four-bedroom townhouse. My son and I had our room; the girls shared a room, and the boys shared a room. My mother had her room.

What a huge change from being with my cousin. Once again, I became the big sister/mother to my siblings. I was now going to a regular high school. The school was a melting pot of mixed races. I felt out of place and kept to myself most of the time. I still felt the shame of having a baby so young. While all the girls my age in school were being cheerleaders, playing sports, and being involved in extracurricular activities, I had to go straight home to my baby.

Some of the girls treated me mean, especially the two girls in my math class. They would call me names, step on the back of my shoe, and bump into me on purpose. I think It was because of how I dressed and looked. I wore a lot of vintage clothes.

My dresses was form-fitting, and I had a very nice shape, almost brick house 36-25-36. Some of the boys would try to talk to me, but I wasn't interested. I had a baby and didn't want another one without being grown and married. But there were these two that were so fine to me that I wished they would say something to me.

All the girls talked about them, "Lonnie and Praxton." Lonnie was light chocolate, had a nice afro, neatly dressed and a head taller than me; he had a smile with nice dimples that would make you melt. He seemed very down to earth, not stuck on himself like Praxton, a senior with a car and apartment.

He was the youngest boy of a well-to-do family, and it just so happened that his apartment was in the same apartment complex mom moved into. He had heard that my mother pressed and curled hair, and he wanted his afro to be pressed. That is when I met him. I would wash and dry people's hair, and my mother would press and curl it with a hot comb and curlers.

When he came to get his hair done, I couldn't believe he was in my house sitting in the chair and my hands were on his head. We talked. He didn't know I went to the same school; why would he? I was a sophomore, and he was a senior. But this was different. He wasn't in school; he was at my house with all that was there: my five siblings and my little man.

Once his hair was pressed, it was very long, making him more handsome to me. He told me he would look out for me in school if he saw me. He wouldn't be a stranger. He kept his word. Every time he saw me in school, he would stop and speak, making the girls hate me more. I must admit I did dress a little revealing. I thought my body was nice, and I showed cleavage and never wore a bra.

Nevertheless, the treatment they gave me wasn't cool. They were jealous, I think; they wanted to look like me because they would always say to me, "You think you cute, yellow bitch." I would tell them, "No, you do; I'm not in your face saying I think I'm cute."

One day, it all endend: "Them bullying me. My mother and I had a fight that morning before school. I was so mad when I got to school. The two mean girls were leaning on my locker. I said excuse me, one of them said move me bitch, if you're bad. Wrong day!

I just grabbed her by the collar and slung her across the hall. Her back hit the edge of the window, and she hit the floor. I turned and told her friend, "Excuse me," and said I would like to get to my locker. She looked at me, stepped aside, and walked across the hall to help her friend up off the floor. I had no more problems with them or anyone else.

To this day, I can't tell you what I and my mother fought about. It was the end of the school year; I did not want to be in school. I didn't think I was learning anything about life and raising a child. I went to my counselor and asked her what I needed to do to get out next year. She signed me up for all the classes I needed to graduate a year ahead of my class.

Praxton saw me in the hall, and I asked him if he was going to his prom. He said he was having a party at his apartment, and I was invited. I was surprised and happy he asked me, especially since his apartment was near my house.

When I got home from school, my mother had a friend at the house, a classmate from down south. She had just moved there and was staying in a nearby apartment complex. She had six children, like my mother: four girls and two boys. She was lovely, dark-skinned, tall, and had a very nice figure for her age to have had six children. She could pass for their sister, not their mother. She looked me up and down, then said how pretty I was and that I needed to meet her children. My mother told her I could take them roller skating on Saturday and she would keep Junior for me.

On Saturday, only her son came, whose name was Marcus. He was about the same age as my brother Junior. We all walked downtown to the local roller skating rink. I wasn't a very good skater. My poor little sister was struggling to go around hanging onto the wall while all the fast, experienced skaters whizzed by her. I couldn't help her I was barely standing on them myself. I went and sat on the bench, and Mike came and sat next to me. He was a friend from Summer Soul School. We talked and caught up on things. He said he was there with his cousin.

As we talked, I noticed they were putting the ropes out so that you could dance in the middle of the rink for the last hour of skating if you didn't want to skate. I was always happy when that time came. I couldn't skate that well, but I knew I could dance. Mike returned our skates to the counter. As I walked to the middle of the rink to the dance floor, I saw my sister and Marcus still skating around on the rink, looking more confident and relieved that there weren't a lot of people skating anymore.

As I stood on the dance floor, someone tapped me on my shoulder and asked if I wanted to dance. I asked them, "First, can you dance?" I did not want to dance with someone who did not know how to dance. He said he could. He could do enough not to look stupid.

As the music played, he asked my name, and I told him. I asked his name, and he said it was Zion. He was dark-skinned, a short fro, and not much taller than me, and had a nice smile and teeth. I don't know why I always look at a person's teeth and their smile. He had a small afro, a long, sharp nose, and dark brown eyes. He was dressed like a white boy, with wrinkled jeans, a tee shirt, and hiking boots.

I wasn't dressed well that night, as I did not want to go, I was still coming out of all the Lamont stuff. My hair wasn't done. I put on the baggiest pants I had and a full blouse. The music stopped, and the lights came on; it was time to go. Zion asked me for my phone number. I pulled out my nickel bag of weed and ripped the top of the envelope out to write my number; he said oh, you get down like that. I said yes, and what? He said that's cool with me.

As we all left the skating rink, Zion and Mike walked behind us; it seemed as if they were following us. They caught up with us, and we talked more; he lived in the same direction, so he asked if he could walk me home. All I could think about was whether the house was clean and if Junior was still up.

We walked and became acquainted. I told him I had a son. His face showed what he wasn't saying. As we reached my house, he walked me to the door, and I opened it so my little sister and Marcus could go in. Surprisingly, the house was clean, and everyone was asleep. Zion asked if he could call me tomorrow; I told him it was okay, and he and his cousin Mike left.

It was prom night for Praxton. He had invited me to his party. My mother was ok with me going because she knew him. I bought the cutest light blue halter top dress that was wrapped around and went past my knees. I wore white candies shoes, my white pearl choker, and small white flowers in my afro. I knew I looked cute; my skin was glowing from the coco butter. I had put on, and I smelled good, too. I was wearing my exclamation cologne. Even my mother complimented me and said I looked nice. I was shocked; she never really said anything nice about me before.

I arrived at the door of Praxton's apartment. I was so excited to be there that I didn't notice there were no extra cars or people hanging outside. I knocked on the door, and he opened the door; all I could do was look at him standing there, tall, pecan tan, nice smile, nice body, smelling good, looking nice in his fitted bell bottom jeans, light blue shirt with navy blueprint design on it. We looked like a couple.

I had never been inside his apartment before; it was nice and clean and decorated very well, had a sofa, television, stereo, coffee table in the living room, dining room table in the dining room. He had drinks and some snacks on the table. I was the only one there; I asked him if it was Too early or too late. He said no, neither you're my only guest.

He told me he liked me and that I looked and smelled nice. He began to tell me that because I was younger than him, he didn't know how I would react to his advances, and I also have a girlfriend. I was forced to date by my family. I knew his family had a lot of influence over his life because he was the youngest. They had multiple businesses and wanted the right girl for him.

I didn't have anything; neither did my family, so why would he even think of me that way as far as to present me to his family? He liked me for more than just doing his hair. He missed his prom with his girlfriend to be with me. I felt so special. I felt butterflies, caterpillars, and everything else inside. Never had anyone made me feel so special like that before. He put some music on, Heatwave; I loved them, Boogie Nights was one of my favorites.

We danced to song after song. We laughed as we got something to drink. He grabbed my hands, looked at me in both my eyes, and said I hope you don't think I'm just saying this, but I really like you a lot. I like your mother, and it doesn't matter to me that you have a baby already. He can be my baby. I didn't know what to say, so I began feeling the caterpillars in my gut change into butterflies.

What do I do with this feeling and the words coming out of his mouth? I wanted to kiss him, and I wanted him to kiss me back, but I didn't want that to lead to other things. I just wanted to know what his lips felt like because the words coming out of his mouth were so sweet to my ears; I knew his lips had to be sweet, too.

I told him that was nice to hear, but I know you have a girlfriend, and I won't be second to anyone. I like you too. Then he kissed me, and I kissed him back. As I did, I felt something so good that it went from my lips to my hips and my privates (if you know what I mean). I was sweating everywhere.

This was new; I had never felt this before. I was suddenly afraid of what might come next. We stopped kissing and went to the living room, where we sat on the sofa. He changed the music, and he played "I'll Be There" by The Four Tops. He said, listening to the words as he sat next to me and put his arm around me, pulling me closer to him. I felt safe with him but afraid of what I was feeling.

When the song ended, he said he would be there for me whenever I needed anything, and then I kissed him. I opened my mouth this time, and we tongue-kissed. I was on fire, and we began to caress each other. I put my hands under his shirt as he began stroking my breast; I knew if I didn't stop, I was going to the point of no return. I never felt this with Lamont.

I never thought about sex after Lamont until now; what am I going to do; this feels so good; I believe he likes me for me. His hand brushed across my nipple that was it. I couldn't hold back anymore. I stopped and told him I couldn't; we needed to stop. He said OK, I want you to be ok. So, we sat, and I shared with him that I didn't like sex and my son's father was the only person I had ever been with, and I was forced into that.

He said he did not want me to be forced into anything, and he did not want to hurt me in any way. Then he asked if he could just hold me in his arms. As I relaxed in his arms, I thought, what a gentleman I didn't want to leave this moment; never have I ever felt this. He told me that when he graduated, he would return to Texas to work in the family business there. He said he would be back for me if I wanted to be with him.

This was too much for one night. I had so many new feelings flowing through my mind and body; I didn't know what to do. We just sat in silence for a while. I knew it was past the time for me to be home. I didn't care. I didn't want this night to end, but I knew if I stayed longer, I might do something I would regret.

I told him I had to go home. It was past the time my mother had told me to be home. He walked me to the door and told me to think about what he had said and that he would see me tomorrow. Then he kissed me on my cheek. He wanted to walk me home. I told him I was ok; I only lived around the corner.

The Next Day

The next day, I could only think about Praxton and last night. I felt like a new person; this handsome, smart senior who all the girls in school liked now wanted me and wanted to be with me. He spent his whole prom night with me, not his girlfriend, and had a party just for me and him. Yet the thought of him leaving after graduation to work in his family business in Texas, which was only a month away, caused sad feelings.

Marcus and his sisters Rita and Jasmine came over, and the knock on the door took my mind away from the thoughts of Praxton leaving. I was happy to see them. We asked some of the other children in the neighborhood if they wanted to play a game of baseball, something we would do on Saturdays and some Sundays. I didn't go to church anymore and haven't gone since living with Aunt V. I can't say I missed going.

Just as we started the game, Zion and his brother Matt came and joined in the game. I remember seeing Matt and this other guy at school. I found out later it was his cousin, who would be dressed to kill and try to get girls to talk to him in the hall. He said he would see me, too. Their sister was a senior and was graduating with Praxton.

Once the game was over, we all bought julips from the candy lady who lived four doors down from us. My team lost the game, Jasmine feared the ball, and Zion caught everything somebody hit. I don't like him. He was short and dressed like a white boy and had a Danny Thomas nose. He was good to get high with he always had some weed.

We all became like a little group that would do things together, like going to the movies, roller skating, and having little cookouts. I would get some of the younger girls and Macus to teach them modern dances.

School was soon to be out. I will be a junior next year, and Praxton will be gone. I talked to my guidance counselor to find out what I needed to do to graduate that year. She signed me up for all the classes I needed to graduate. I was so happy cause I didn't feel like school was teaching me anything about real life, but I didn't want to drop out.

I saw Praxton down the hall as I came out of the counselor's office. I did and didn't want him to see me; I turned the other way so he would see my back and stood there until I thought he would be gone. He was in my face when I turned around, and the butterflies started. He smiled and said hi, gave me a folded piece of paper, and said he would be over later. The bell rang for the next class. I told him OK and rushed to my class, putting the folded paper in my pocket.

The class was boring as usual. I did what I needed to do in each class to satisfy the teacher for a good grade. I couldn't concentrate after seeing Praxton. After school, I rushed to catch my bus home; the minute I got in the door, my mother said here, take your baby. She did not give me a break when it came to taking care of my baby. She would always say, "So long as you are in school, I'll take care of him, but the minute you out, get your baby."

It was ok. I love my little Junior; I would do my homework before doing anything else, and he would be in the room with me, playing or just sitting. He was a good baby. Sometimes, my brothers or sisters would want to take him until he needed a dirty diaper changed.

Just as I finished my homework, the doorbell rang; my mother called and said someone was there for me. I looked down the stairs and saw the front door from the top of the stairs. It was Praxton. I came downstairs carrying Junior on my hip. He smiled and said hi to Junior, then asked if I would step outside for a minute. I did.

He asked if I had read the note he had given me. I had forgotten about it. I reached into my pocket, opened the note, and began to read it. It was asking me to come to his apartment on graduation night and gave me the time and his phone number. I told him I would have to call and let him know later.

The graduation was next Friday. I needed to make sure I had a babysitter, the school would be out, and I'm sure he didn't want me to bring him with me even though I didn't ask.

Praxton made me feel so special. I wanted to just be around him, and it would be even better if that was being alone with him. He made me feel safe and loved. School is almost over, and the summer is here, one more week than Friday.

I went to my Cousin Joy's house and took Junior with me for the night. I liked going to Joy's. She was someone who treated me special, too. When I got there, the music was playing. Her door was open, but the screen door was closed and locked. I could see the light coming out her door and hear New Birth's album playing. She loved them. Joy had a very nice apartment, clean and well-kept. I saw her dancing to the music when I knocked on the door.
She opened the door and let me in; a card game was going on at the kitchen table, and some of her friends were in the

living room having drinks and grooving to the music. I put Junior down next to Joy's youngest daughter, who was about the same age as Junior.

I started to dance to the music, my back was facing the door to the bathroom. When I turned around, who did I see, Lamont? I was surprised to see him. He smiled and said hi. I missed him. He went and got Junior and held him the whole time, talking and playing with him.

I looked across the room at him, trying not to let him know I was looking. He looked like he had this glow all around him, especially his face. Everybody kept saying, "Lamont, man, you look good." I could see that he did. I thought to myself, "He is fine. I loved the way he walked."

Before he got ready to leave, he asked if we could talk. I told him we could, so we sat on the step-in front of Joy's apartment. It was dark, and the moon and stars were shining so bright that they lit up the sky. Lamont still seemed to have this beautiful glow; he appeared very handsome to me. In the back of my mind, I wanted to be a family, and I wanted my son to have what I didn't: a father in his life.

I had expected Lamont to want the same things. He said he missed me and was so sorry for hitting me. He said that he had seen his older brother and thought that was how to keep our girl in line, but he knew it was wrong and asked if I would please give him one more chance.

I don't know why, but he looked so good, and the glow around him was unexplainable. Junior and I were supposed to stay at Joy's, but I went home; Lamont came and stayed the night. I had snuck him into my room. For the first time, I wanted to have sex with him. This was different; he was gentler. I could feel a genuine sense of care, gentleness, or even love, something I didn't know. Except I knew I loved my son.

Lamont snuck out of the back patio door before everyone got up. I told him I would call him later because I might bring Junior over while my mother and I go shopping. Lamont and I were back together again, and last night was good. After all, we may become a family; if I have more children, they will have the same father.

I couldn't go to sleep after Lamont left. I was still high and had the munchies, so I looked for some food, made a peanut butter and jelly sandwich, poured a glass of milk, and took it to my room. Junior was still asleep.

I couldn't stop thinking about how good Lamont looked and that glow. I finished my food and drifted off to sleep when my mother knocked on the door, calling my name. As she opened it, she said, "You still going with me?" She continued to come into my room. I am sure she could smell the weed and sex, but she dared not say anything about it because she didn't want me to go off on her. I had no genuine respect for my mother. I didn't think she really cared for me. She was more like a sister. I had a love-hate relationship with her. The little girl in me loved and missed her, but the now teenager hated her.

As I got up, she left the room. She was already dressed. I took a bath and dressed myself before waking Junior to dress him. When I got in the car, I told my mother I was going to take Junior to Lamont so he could watch him while we shopped. As we pulled up to the apartments where Lamont lived with his brother, I felt something in the pit of my stomach and heard, "Don't leave him. "I told my mother I'm not going to leave Junior. I'm taking him with us. She wasn't happy and told me to make up my mind. I just said I'm taking him with us.

After shopping, we pulled into the parking lot of the apartment complex where we lived; my sister came running to the car and was talking loudly and fast. At first, I didn't understand what she was saying, but by the third time, when she calmed down, I understood. She said Lamont's mother came over and told her Lamont was in a fire and was burnt badly. My heart dropped. I gave Junior to my sister and my mother, and I went to the hospital.

When we got there, Lamont's mother greeted us in the intensive care burn unit hall. A nurse came out of the room. I asked if I could see him. She told me I could, but he is not going to look like himself and won't be able to respond, but he can hear you. She gave me a gown, gloves, and head covering and told me I needed to wear them because his skin was open and exposed; he couldn't get any germs or infections.

When I walked into the room, the noise from all the machines was deafening; he had tubes everywhere. When I looked at him, his head was swollen to the size of a basketball, and his face was burnt and red with blisters. I almost passed out; I thought I had to be strong. I said with tears in my eyes and pain and fear in my voice, "Lamont, I'm here".

I repeated, "Lamont, I'm here." I saw a slight movement as I looked down at his hand, even though his hands were bandaged. 47% of his body was burned including his face. You could only visit for fifteen minutes at a time.

As I left the room, I remembered the times he would hit me and tell me to jump bitch you bad I would just say I don't have to get you; God's going to get you and I would quote one of the scriptures I remembered from Sunday School Romans 12:13 "Vengeance is mine, I will repay." I said God, you didn't have to do it like this.

I was grateful that he didn't die, but I instantly thought if I had taken Junior and left him, he might be dead now. I think I know what it means to listen to your gut. I don't know what I would have done if Junior had been in that fire, too. I cared that Lamont was burnt. I had a newfound love for him and wanted him to live.

I was at the hospital every day after school, talking to him and letting him know I was there. Lamont was in the hospital for three months. The first month, he was in a medically induced coma; the second month, they woke him up. They said they had to wake him so they would know how much movement he had on his own and if he could breathe on his own. The third month was physical therapy, learning to talk, walk, breathe, use his hands, and eat again.

During the third month, I came to the hospital, and they told me that he wouldn't do anything that day because he saw himself for the first time since the fire. They warned me of his attitude and state of mind before I went in to see him. I had accepted what he would look like for the rest of his life. I didn't care about what he looked like on the outside; I knew who he was inside.

When I went into the room and said hi, he didn't respond. I told him if he didn't help himself get better and work with the medical people, I would not come back to the hospital. I told him I didn't care what he looked like. I still loved him and wanted us to be a family, but if he didn't, I'm too young to keep coming here being with someone who doesn't want to have the same things.

I told him people may look at you, but they don't know you, and you don't know them, so why care what others think as long as we have each other? Then I left. I was tired. I felt like my time was wasted coming to the hospital every day and going to school tired and sleepy.

The next day, I returned to the hospital; the nurse met me at the door to Lamont's room and said, "Whatever you said to him yesterday worked; he has been working very hard today doing everything the therapist, and we ask him to do." I was so happy to hear that.

When I went in, he had a big smile on his face. He was feeding himself. It was the first time I saw him do that since he started therapy. His hands were burned, and they had to strap a spoon or fork to them. I told him I was proud of him and now know he wants to live. After three months, Lamont was released from the hospital to do the basics of taking care of himself. He would go back from time to time for skin graft surgeries. His skin was still healing. His arms and face were the worst.

When we walked down the street together, people would stare. He knew they were staring, and some even seemed afraid, like my younger sister. They would always run and hide, except my youngest sister, Bob. She would talk to him and treat him like she remembered him before.

I would have to continue encouraging him that I loved him and that what others think and do doesn't matter. I was too young to consider putting myself in his place. How would I feel? I hoped that by being there with him through it all, he would get it and come to a place of living in his world and my world, not the outside world.

One Friday night, Lamont came over; my mother and her friends were going out, and I planned for Junior and me to spend the night at my aunt's house. Lamont wants me to stay there with him. I told my aunt I would help her with something, and she was expecting me. Lamont got very angry and pushed me into the closet in my room and started to hit me, and before I realized it, I had scratched both his arms where the skin had not healed and ran down the stairs where my mother and friend were waiting to drop me off to my aunt's house.

Lamont followed, cursing, calling my mother's friend all kinds of nasty names, and kicking his car. My mother tried calming him down, but he wouldn't listen. I got in the car with Junior, and we left him in the parking lot.

That was it; I couldn't do this anymore. I had no tears to cry. I felt hurt, angry, and embarrassed. I didn't say anything the whole way to my aunts. When I got home the next day, he called me, saying he was sorry; he just wanted to be with Junior and me.

I was done. I told him that I wanted us to be a family and that I couldn't do the hitting and cursing anymore. I will be here for you as a mother to our son but not as a girlfriend, and you can get and see Junior whenever you want; I will not stop you from seeing him. Then I hung up the phone.

I cried inside and out for days, not only because of the breakup but now my son won't have a life with a father and mother together, loving and raising him. I did not want Junior to see his father hitting his mother or calling her a bitch. That night, I saw the old Lamont and wanted no part of him.

Now here I am, lying next to Praxton and thinking of all this. Graduation night was here, and Praxton would leave for Texas next week. When I came to his apartment, I knew I might go all the way with him. I was feeling him, and I felt like he really liked me and was coming back for me and Junior.

I entered the door and heard the music in the living room playing; instantly, I felt like dancing. I had smoked a joint before and drank a wine cooler. I was feeling nice. Praxton didn't get high, and he didn't seem to care that I did. I wouldn't do it in front of or around him. Marvin Gaye's album was playing the song "Got to Give It Up."

I gave it up for sure; Praxton was very gentle it was over so fast. I didn't feel him inside me; I knew it was out but I didn't feel him like, I would Lamont. I hope I don't get pregnant again. We didn't use any protection, and I didn't take the pills they gave me because they made me gain weight, although a baby would too.

Praxton just looked at me with a look of satisfaction and awe. He told me I was beautiful, and my skin glowed in the dark. He promised that it wasn't a one-night thing and that he would return. I felt so loved and wanted.

He hasn't lied to me; he has done everything he said he would do before he left. Praxton gave me money and told me to use it for whatever Junior and I needed. "I'm coming back for you" were his last words to me after a long kiss goodbye. For some reason, I believed him. However, I didn't forget he had a girlfriend his family wanted him to be with.

Summer Vacation

The school year ended, and we were out for the summer. I was thrilled to visit my Grand-ma-ma; she would see her great-grandson for the first time. I was a little ashamed to see her face-to-face. I was sure she wasn't proud that I had a baby. Oh my God what are all the folk in her church going to say? I know they've all been talking. I can't imagine what Titus will say or think of me when he sees me and his grandson and making him a grandfather so young.

Part of me didn't care what anyone thought, Junior is mine, and he isn't going anywhere, and people will talk anyway. They don't know what he really means to me. I love my Grand-ma-ma, and what she thinks and how she will treat me now matters to me.

The ride from New York to the small southern town was long and hot; traveling with a little baby seemed even longer. I always knew when we were close when we stopped for gas and to use the bathroom, the people talked very country, and some whites weren't friendly. Once we were on Highway 10, I knew it was a matter of maybe an hour before we reached my Grand-ma-ma's house.

I always felt happy every time I came back down south. I loved the peace there, playing in the yard amongst the fruit and pecan trees and with her younger sisters who lived next door. Memories of childhood flooded my mind.

My mother drove her big burgundy Buick all the way. She stopped once to rest and let us leave the car, eat, and use the bathroom. I am happy finally to be parking in front of my Grand-ma-ma's house.

She was at the door waiting for us, to get out of the car. I could smell the food coming from her kitchen; she would always have hot food ready for anyone traveling from out of state to see her and my aunt did the same when people would come from the south to the north.

We all gave her a hug and piled up on her porch. Grand-ma-ma asked to see the baby. It was so hot he just had on a diaper and a sleeveless cotton tank shirt. One of my sisters was holding him, she gave Junior to her, and she smiled and said he is a fine little boy, handsome. He looks good to have been so small when he was born. "He looks like he is being taken care of. I am proud of you for that," she said.

I know y'all are hungry and want to get a bath. My mother went into the house to take a bath. The girls took theirs together, then the boys. Junior fell asleep in my Grand-ma-ma's arms, so I took my bath while he was asleep. Because we weren't going to sit at her table dirty or smelly.

When I came out of the bathroom, Junior was still asleep; everyone else was eating, and except for my mother, she was already asleep on the couch. She had eaten while I was in the bathroom. I'm sure she was tired from driving all the way.

The food was so good I loved my Grand-ma-ma's cooking. She had cooked red beans, rice, fried chicken, barbeque chicken, greens, and cornbread. She had fresh cucumber, tomato, and red onion salad from her garden. She made a lemon-glazed pound cake. Her pound cakes were the best; everyone paid her to make them one.

I ate so much that my stomach hurt; I could barely move. I sat on the porch like a slopped-drunk hog. My sisters and brothers were playing in the yard. I sat watching them and enjoying the peace I felt just being there on my Grand-ma-ma's porch; as the evening sun went down to make room for the moon, the sky had the most beautiful colors you didn't see in the north.

The days were moving too fast for me; my Uncle Beard was here from New Orleans with his wife and children. The first thing he asked me "have you seen your daddy?" Sadly, I had not, but I wanted him to see his grandson.

I am sure he knew I was there; small towns talk. Maybe he was ashamed of me. In the past, when I would come down, he called me and came by my Grand-ma-ma's house. He would always give me money. I was sure my uncle was going to his house, even if just for a haircut, and he didn't have any hair on his head. He was going to make sure Titus knew I was in town.

I loved my Uncle Beard and Aunt May; I stayed with them when they came to live in New York. Auntie May made the best popcorn balls. I would visit them in New Orleans when I came down. One summer, while visiting, I was hanging out with their neighbor's son, Burt, and his friends.

We went to one of his friends' houses to get high, and they rolled a joint and gave it to me and said bust it up, so I broke it up. They were like girl, what are you doing? I said, "I busted it up. You want me to reroll it." They cracked up laughing and they said, "No! Girl, smoke it. I told them, "We say fire it up!" I felt so stupid; the feeling soon passed as I lit the newly rolled joint. I don't know where they got that weed, but it was good.

I was high off one draw. We had good times together. I loved getting the freshly made honey buns from the bakery across the street from my uncle's house. I and Auntie May would sit on the steps waiting for them to open. We would get them right as the door opened; they were warm, soft, gooey, and honey-sweet and melted in our mouths.

My cousin Biscuit lived in New Orleans, and one year, I visited. He came to pick me up in this old vintage Ford pickup truck; it was a classic. We rode around New Orleans drinking Jack Daniels. I was so drunk by the time I got out of that truck that I didn't know how he was able to drive, maybe because he loved cars and drove fast. He lived and breathed cars.

My cousin Biscuit was somewhat of a rebel. I loved him and being with him; I called him Biscuit because when he came to Aunt V's house, his mother, he would eat biscuits hot out of the oven and would eat the whole pan if she'd let him.

I don't know what he did to Uncle Beard, but I stood between my Uncle Beard and a loaded gun he was holding, wanting to kill Biscuit. I'll never forget that day. Biscuit did a lot of rebellious stuff. Still, to this day, I don't know why, but my uncle never shot him. What memories.

Friends and family members often asked me if I saw my daddy. Does he know you're here? His wife would just ask how long I was down for; I didn't like them asking me about him.

They didn't know I wanted to see him more than they wanted to know if I saw him. Not only did I want to see him I wanted to be a part of his life. I wanted to know my other sisters and brother. I wanted them to love me not just know about me. Now, they have a nephew. My uncle, I'm sure, means well.

The time was going so fast; there was only one more day with Grand-ma-ma. Last night was fun, all my uncles and aunts and their children were here at my Grand-ma-ma's house. I admired and wanted what they had: mother and father, a real family, "You know." Even though I was with my mother, sisters, and brothers, I was more like their mother and my mother like an older sister. I had to make sure she kept a roof over our heads and food to eat.

Even though I didn't care for my mother as I should have. I didn't like the way her siblings treated her they treated her like she was not a part of them. My Grand-ma-ma treated her differently sometimes, too. I also noticed how the grandchildren of her younger children were treated better or with a little more kindness than her older children's children.

It was Sunday. Everyone was getting ready for church, some going to Sunday school, others coming later for regular Sunday Service at the local church my Grand-ma-ma attended. This was the same church my father and his family went to, and I prayed I would see him.

During church service, I had to take Junior out to the car; I wanted to change him. Who do I see in the parking lot? There he stood, tall and handsome, with a smile and a mouth full of gold. My daddy! He saw me and followed me to the car. I hugged him once I changed Junior's diaper. He asked to hold Junior then said, "Fine boy, I'm a grandfather."

I was so happy; he didn't hate me or make me feel shameful. He asked how I had been doing and if I needed anything. I really couldn't think. I was so happy that he was standing in front of me. I felt the hole beginning to fill my heart, which I didn't realize was there until this very moment.

I wanted to say, "I need you!" But all I said was I was good. He gave me money anyway and told me he loved me. I stayed in the car and didn't go back into the church. He went in, and one of his daughters came out. It was as if he didn't want her to see me talking to him.

When church service was over, I got out of the car to speak to some of the family I knew and classmates from when I went to school there. When I saw Titus's wife, she smiled and said "hello" and asked me how long I was down for; I told her we would be leaving tomorrow. She smiled and said, "This your baby?" I had Junior on my hip, "I heard you had a baby, cute little fellow."

Something inside of me didn't feel right when she spoke to me. It felt like she wasn't genuine. I thought she was pretty. She had dark, smooth skin and a beauty mark on her nose. Her daughters were standing next to her, but they didn't speak. She said it was nice seeing you, take care of that baby, and have a safe trip back north. I couldn't quite put my finger on what I was feeling when around her; I didn't like it.

After church, we had dinner. My mother wanted to load the car up because we were leaving before daybreak. She wanted to get more daylight driving in, especially in the southern states. After we loaded the car and everyone had their baths, I sat on the porch to watch the sun go down and wished I could see my father again. Just as I got up to walk into the house, a red pickup truck pulled into the lane. I didn't recognize it. I waited on the porch until whoever got out and came to the screen door of the porch.

Two men got out of the truck. Wow! It was my father and his brother, my uncle. His name was Preston. Titus said he wanted Preston to see me and the baby. Preston looked at me, smiled, and, low and behold, gold teeth just like my father. He didn't have as much gold as my dad, though.

He asked me if I remembered when I was younger, and he took me to meet their mother, my other grandmother, before she died. I remember her having a small picture of me on her wall in the kitchen. You look good and have a fine baby boy. We went into the house where everyone else was, and they spoke to everyone, then said they weren't going to stay long but stayed for a good while talking.

When they got up to leave, I walked them to the truck. Uncle Preston gave me some money, hugged me, kissed me on the cheek, and said, "Take care of that baby." My dad hugged me so tight and said, "I love you, and you are mine." They got into the truck, backed it up, and turned it around in the yard. I stood there watching until he drove out of the lane and down the road, and I couldn't see the taillights anymore.

Once again, my heart ached and longed for family and for him to be in my life every day, but that was not going to happen; by this time next week, I'll be back in New York, and he'll be here with his family.

On the way back, all I could think about was the time spent with my Grand-ma-ma and seeing my father. As we pulled into the parking lot of our apartment complex, my mind went to Praxton. Had he moved yet?

After we took everything out of the car, I walked around the corner to his apartment, knocked on the door, and this girl opened the door. My heart sank. I asked if Praxton was there.

She said he didn't live there anymore; she said she moved in as he moved out last week. I thanked her and walked away feeling so sad I wanted to see him again before he left.

When I got home, everybody was asleep, even Junior stretched out on the floor in the living room. I went to my room, rolled a joint, and smoked it, blowing the smoke out of my bedroom window. So, the smell wouldn't linger in my room.

As I lay on my bed feeling nice, enjoying the peace and quiet, my mind began to recall the events of the trip down south and Praxton being gone. This is going to be a long summer.

We all slept through the night; the doorbell woke me up. Marcus, Verna's son, came for the stuff my mother had brought back for her. He told me he had been hanging out with Zion, and he was asking when we would be back. He said he would see him later and tell him we were back. I told him it was okay and that we could get a baseball game going if he came back.

We all hung out playing baseball, skating, and watching movies throughout the summer. Zion was teaching me karate and how to use the nun chucks. We went swimming at the local recreation center; he would show off his diving skills by doing flips and all kinds of dives.

Sometimes, Zion would take Junior when I needed a babysitter or just for Junior to hang out with the boys. I thought that was something special, and he seemed to care about Junior, which made me look at him differently. I still didn't like him as a boyfriend. I was not going to allow him in that place. I still believed Praxton was coming back. I made sure Zion knew about my feelings. He didn't know about Praxton. No one did.

Summer was over, and the new school year had started. I was happy to be a senior. I will miss seeing Praxton in the halls and meeting him after school.

My periods have been funny ever since sleeping with him. I had two pregnancy tests, and they said I'm not pregnant; something is wrong. I did have a period this month, but my stomach is hard, and my breasts are sore. I'm going to wait one more month. If it's not here, I'm going to get checked again. God, please don't let me be pregnant. I have no way of getting in touch with Praxton and don't need another baby now.

I went to the teen clinic to be rechecked and received news I did not want to hear. The doctor said I was four and a half months pregnant. How could that be? I had my period for two months and a spotty one for one month. God, what am I going to do? I can't tell my mother; I can't tell anybody. Two babies, and I'm only in my teens.

The next day, I went to my guidance counselor and told her what was happening. I told her I didn't tell anyone and didn't know how to contact the father. All I could think about was another baby without a father in its life.

The counselor asked me if I was going to continue the pregnancy. If not, she could make arrangements for me to terminate. I didn't know what to do. I knew I didn't want another baby without Praxton. The counselor said I would need to get the Medicaid card from my mother, and I would be away for a few days because I was so far along it would have to be terminated at a medical facility.

I felt horrible. Everything inside me cringed; she was talking about an abortion. She convinced me that everything was going to be ok. She reminded me that I was only in my teens and about to have another baby with no father in the picture. I didn't want that or the embarrassment. Not to mention, Praxton didn't know, and he had a girlfriend.

When I got home, I lied and told my mother that some seniors would visit a college campus next weekend, and I needed the Medicaid card to show I had health insurance. She believed me. That Friday, my counselor gave me the information, and I took the city bus to the hospital and was admitted.

Lost and Found

The nurse at the desk didn't ask for a parent; this part of the hospital seemed cold and dreary, and I had no feelings for some reason. Two nurses showed me to my room with a hospital bed and a chair and told me to undress, take everything off, and put on the hospital gown that they handed me.

They hooked me up to an IV and told me it was the saline solution and that it was going to cause me to go into premature labor. I didn't understand all of what they were telling me. Now I was scared, now I'm thinking, what if I die nobody will know I'm here? I'm sure my counselor won't tell them because she didn't say anything to my mother or tell me to let anyone know I was going to be there.

I watched the drops of solution drip into the IV, counting one by one until I drifted off to sleep, only to be awakened by the worst pain I had ever felt in my life, worse than when I had Junior. Then I felt an urge to push like I was having a bowel movement.

I pushed the button for the nurse, but I couldn't hold it, and before I knew it, a scream came out of my mouth, and a big blob came out of my vagina. The nurse grabbed it and ran out of the door, and another nurse cleaned me up. Everything happened so fast I couldn't think. I just had a baby, but I didn't hear it cry. God, what have I done? I'm so stupid; all kinds of self-destructive thoughts raced through my mind.

The nurse was saying something to me, but I wasn't listening; I couldn't hear her through the many voices now shouting in my head. I wanted to get high. I needed some peace; God help me!!! What have I done?

They let me stay there until the next day; they said they wanted to make sure I did not have any adverse reaction to the medicine and no extra bleeding. I wanted to run out of that place and never see it again.

When I got home, my mother asked why I returned so early; she thought I was gone until Sunday. I told her I got my period and didn't want to stay. I had to go on as if nothing had happened. I had to get my mind right; I got Junior, took him to my room with me, held him, and cried; he seemed to know something was wrong. He just laid with me and patted my back. I thank God I didn't do this to him. I will never tell a soul.

On Monday, the counselor called me to her office to see if I was okay and how things were going. I just said, "OK, I'm good," knowing I was a wreck inside. I told her all I wanted to do was focus on getting out of school and going on with my life.

She asked what I wanted to do when I graduated. I told her I might go into the Air Force or work as a Juvenile Probation Officer. She said she would look into that to see which one fit me better. A part of me hated this lady, and another could not blame her because I had made the choice.

It was hard to focus on school, and at home, the event continued to replay in my mind. I couldn't get the vision of the nurse picking up what came out of me and running out of the room. I believe it was my baby that didn't cry. All I wanted to do was die, and I couldn't do that because I had Junior to live for. I didn't want him not to have me, his mother, in his life.

I would pray to God, hoping He would hear me and forgive me for what I had done. Not feeling any release, I started smoking more weed and taking acid pills only on the weekend because I would trip so hard. I wanted to finish school. I would tell myself get over it, it's over, forget it, it's over, you can't bring it back, you must move on; no one knows but you, God, the counselor, and the hospital staff.

I was happy the holidays were coming, and I'll have a break from school. The memories of seeing Praxton in the hall and seeing the counselor didn't help me move on. Every time the counselor saw me, she would have this look of pity on her face, like she felt bad about it, too. I need this break from school.

My aunt called to tell me my father had sent me something for Christmas. Hearing that made me happy; I told her I would be over on Sunday. I needed him, not his gifts. Maybe I would have made many different choices if he had been here, and my mother had known me, showed me she loved me, and had not given me away.

Now I think she tolerates me because of the extra money and food stamps having me and Junior live with her. I didn't care. At least I was with her and my sisters and brothers, who looked up to me more than they did her most times. I was the one they came to when they were hungry and wanted to go outside to play or bring someone over.

My mother spent most of her time working or hanging out with her friends. She would buy the food and cook sometimes. I was the mother figure for real! They looked up to me. Even though I had more responsibility than living with Aunt V, I wouldn't turn back the hands of time they loved and needed me.

Sunday was here, and Aunt V still cooked the best dinners and desserts. Some of her friends from church were there. I loved talking to them and just watching them interact with each other. Sister Annie was my favorite. She talked slowly and steadily and ate her food the same way. She would make funny remarks but very serious ones. She dressed with everything coordinating and matching. She walked statuesque, and her Sunday hats made her look taller than she was.

This Sunday was special because I was getting something from my father. The thought of him made me smile wider and brighter, his last words replaying, "I love you, and you are mine."

After dinner and after we had cleaned the kitchen, my aunt gave me an envelope with my name on it. She said, "Your father sent this to you for Christmas." I thanked her. As we walked out of her room, Sister Annie was saying her goodbyes; with her hat and leftovers in hand, everyone always took food home. Soon after, Junior and I left, too. I didn't open the envelope until I got home and went into my room because I knew they would be asking me what he had sent, and I didn't want to tell them. I felt that was between him and I.

I opened the envelope I saw the money in the middle of the Christmas card. I was thankful but had no way to tell him that; I couldn't just call him or say hey, Dad, I got your gift. Thank you so much. I just went on as always, wishing I had him, not the money; however, I could still use the money.

During the holidays, the crew still went skating and to the movies. I hated walking in the snow. Zion didn't care, but Marcus and I would be freezing. The north winter can be mean, and the hawk doesn't care. It will whip across your body like a samurai sword cutting through you. And Jack Frost will bite your nose, feet, toes, and hands, leaving you with a pain that never seems to end.

Some days, we walked to the movies, and there would be no snow, nice clean streets, and sidewalks; when we came out, it looked like hell had broken loose, snow blowing everywhere. I didn't like winter in the north.

Marcus and I were from the south, a warm place that did not snow. Zion was born in this mess. I was thankful my house wasn't far from downtown, where the movie theater and the Roller Palace were. After reaching my house, I didn't even say goodbye to Marcus or Zion; they had a little further to go before getting home. On this Sunday night, I swore I would not go out in the winter anymore, only to school. I was so cold.

I knew once the holidays were over, it was closer to the time for me to finish school. I began to focus more as the days went by, and I knew I had to pass every class. Ms. Millie, who lived some door down from me, told me I'd better get that diploma. I would stop at her house some mornings to bum a cigarette from her, then try to stay there for the day. She would cuss me out, push me out of her house, and tell me to go get it. I love you, Ms. Millie, is all I would say with your skinny self. Ms. Millie helped to keep me focused, but she didn't even know it.

As the days continued, Zion and I spent more time together hanging out after school. Zion had dropped out of school. One day, after walking home from the movies, he walked me to the door of my house and then came in. He stood near the door, grabbed my hand, looked at me, and said he was falling in love with me. I snatched my hand away and said, please don't. I didn't want to get involved with anyone else.

And I was thinking of Lamont, who was in the hospital again for more surgery and skin grafts; he is still Junior's father. In a way, I still had hope. Praxton was gone, and I wasn't sure he would return. All this ran through my mind at that moment. I don't have it in me right now. So, I told him again not to fall in love with me. I told him to go back to school or something and then told him to leave.

Everyone who claims to love me doesn't; how do I know what love is or looks like? I only knew that what I felt for Junior had to be real. What I feel for Titus, I know, was real. I don't feel any of that for Zion.

I like him, but as a friend, I want someone to hang out with, get high with, and play cards and stuff. He seemed to really like Junior and spent time with him. I'm still trying to understand if that is love.

One day after school, I went to visit Lamont. When I got home, Zion had left a letter for me. In the letter, he continued to confess his love for me and said, at the end, "If your heart is at the hospital, you need to stay there." I don't know what it was, but something about those words changed my feelings for him.

Lamont was always happy to see I still cared, and he would always say he would get me back, but those words on paper from Zion seemed final, like I would never see him again and Junior wouldn't have him in his life anymore.

When I went to the hospital the next day, I told Lamont I was going to start seeing someone else. He just turned his head and said I understand. Then, he proceeded to tell me not to come back.

I called Zion when I got home and asked him to come over. We needed to be face-to-face with what I wanted to tell him. Everyone had gone with my mother to the store when Zion arrived. We sat in the living room, and he looked at me and said, "What? I told him my heart wasn't at the hospital, I do have feelings for you that I am still working through. Tell me this: how could you walk away from Junior like that? He jokingly answered, "My mama said if you want the cow, you must take the calf, too." I just smiled. I knew what she meant.

His facial expression became very stern as he looked at me and said he couldn't continue coming over to hang out, knowing how he felt about me, that I didn't feel the same way, and that I wouldn't even give us a chance. What is your mother going to say? What does she think about me already having a baby? These are questions I asked him.

He told me he had already talked to her about me, and she just said, "You know you would have a ready-made family, and why don't you like the girls at the church who don't have any children?" She even had all her brothers talk to me, he told me.

He said he was thinking about joining the Navy. I told him I was thinking of going into the Air Force, and my counselor was looking into it for me. I had to decide before May. We talked about our future and what we wanted.

Zion and I are now boyfriend and girlfriend, even though I wasn't sure about being in a relationship after everything I had been through. We spent a lot of time together. What we had in common was our enjoyment of smoking weed together and eating after.

Then there was the sex. The first time wasn't what I expected. I was high and a little tipsy, and my body wanted to do it. It's something how you become a different person when you are high or drunk. It's like you just let it flow. I made sure I took my birth control pills. I did not want to get pregnant again.

Zion got a job at a department store. He seemed happy initially, but after some time, he didn't enjoy the job as much and realized he was not making much money. So, he decided it was best for him to go into the Navy. It was official after taking the test, passing the physical exam, and receiving the date to leave for basic training. He was ready.

His mother was giving him a going away party. I wasn't invited, but Zion came and got me to bring me to the party. When we got there, another girl from his church that liked him. I'm sure she was invited. I didn't feel welcomed by his family.

I thought about what his mother said and felt the shame of being so young with a baby, knowing what they might be thinking, "I don't know why Zion wants to be with me." Maybe he thought I was easy because I had a baby. I don't know, but I'm with him, and he brought me to his party to meet his family.

We didn't stay at the party long. Zion could tell I wasn't comfortable. When we returned to my house that night, he asked me if I would wait for him. I told him I would. He was leaving for training the next day; we spent most of the night together. The thought of him being away made me feel more deeply for him, and I knew I would miss him. He told me he would write as often as possible, and we could talk on weekends when he called his mother's house.

Another shift in my life to adjust to. Will he come back? I had to get my mind back on graduating and decide what to do after.

About three weeks after Zion left for training, I got a letter saying he really missed Junior and me and that someday he wanted to marry me. He said, "Since he was in the Navy, I should not go into the Air Force because it would be harder for us to be together."

Little did he know I didn't pass the physical exam for the Air Force. They said it was because I had flat feet and teeth missing in the back, so I didn't qualify. So, I decided to attend college to become a Juvenile Probation Officer. I had a heart for teens. I felt older than I was and more mature, and I'm sure it was because of all the things I had already experienced. I didn't like how some of us were labeled after making mistakes or being exposed to bad things. There was something in me that always wanted to see people smile and be happy, and if I could be a part of that happening, sign me up.

I took the college entrance exam but didn't score high enough. "I was crushed." I didn't want to end up like most of the young mothers around my neighborhood, living on welfare, waiting for the first and sixteenth of the month for the government to send them a check and food stamps, and then being in all your financial business. I didn't want that, but it started to look like I might become one of them. I didn't know what to do now. I was not sure if I Should get a job or something.

Graduation Day quickly approached, and all I could say was that I made it. I was so happy to see my name in the program and my picture in the yearbook as a senior. I wanted to look different, so my mother cut my hair into a cute bob. I loved it.

I ensured Ms. Millie came; she had to be there when they called my name, and I walked up on the stage to get a diploma that meant so much to me. I knew that when I walked off that stage my life would begin anew.

After the ceremony, Ms. Millie hugged me and told me, "You did it, girl." My mother looked at me with a look of pride on her face. Ms. Millie said, "You not going to hug your daughter?" I reached and hugged her, but she kind of cringed. I didn't care; I graduated. When I got home, I grabbed Junior, held him tight, and said, "Mommy did it." He seemed to be happy to see his mommy happy.

My sisters and brothers were happy for me. I went to a graduation party with other graduates and had so much fun. I didn't get home until the next day. I had gotten so high I fell asleep at my girlfriend's house. It was good for me that my mother slept hard, and I got in before she woke up. Junior was still asleep with my little sister. They didn't know when I got in. I stayed up thinking about what I was going to do now; I was an adult at sixteen.

Monday morning, my mother and I went to the rental office of the apartment complex we lived in. She asked the manager if any two-bedroom apartments were available. They did have one; she said my daughter needed it. I also needed to get help from welfare, so we went to the welfare office. It was so packed. The receptionist said I would have to come back later. It was okay because the apartment wouldn't be available right away anyway.

I'm sure Mother was tired of me and my disrespect. She did what she needed to do to help get me out of school and now to get me out of her house. I would hear older women, who came to Aunt V's house for Sunday dinner, saying, "Two grown women can't live in the house together." I guess I was grown now, and it was time to be on my own. My mother made sure we did everything to make that happen.

I was going to be in my own apartment, which would be ready on September 1st. I was going to be a welfare mother like so many in the neighborhood. I wasn't feeling that at all. I was only sixteen and will now be in this big world learning to answer to myself and raise my son.

My mother told me what I needed to do when I went to the welfare office. When I got there, it was packed; the line was out the door at seven in the morning. This was all new to me; some of the people looked homeless and depressed. There were young girls with their babies; there were just as many people inside as outside. I was called to see someone thirty minutes before the office closed. They gave me a bunch of papers with everything I would need to return.

The lady behind the desk seemed nice. After she told me how it all worked, I told her to give me one year of help because I did not want to be on welfare. She smiled and looked at me as if to say, "That's what you think." She told me what I would get for me and Junior once my paperwork was handed in.

She also told me the only reason I could get this assistance was because of my baby. I told her that was also why I would only need it for one year. I was determined not to be a welfare mom. I did not want my son to be a part of the cycle. I wanted him to have a family. I wanted him to see a mother and father go to work, not sit around day in and day out, getting high, drinking, and waiting on a check from the government. But for now, I will take what I can to help me until I can help myself.

The summer went by so fast. I couldn't wait to move out of my mother's house next week. I was afraid and excited all at the same time. I was scared of failing and leaving my brothers and sisters behind to fend for themselves, But I was excited because I'd be in my own apartment and have no one to answer to or clean up after. No coming home to a dirty house, No food, and No toilet paper. I can keep my house like I want it. I can smoke weed when I want to and drink my wine coolers openly. I'm going to be free.

When moving day came, I didn't have much to move: my bed, which Auntie Em bought me when I lived with her, my clothes, and Junior's clothes. My mother gave me her red sofa and end tables. I was in my apartment, around the corner from my mother, sisters, and brothers.

I liked where my apartment was. From my living room window, I could see the playground. From my bedroom window, I could see the front of the building, so I would know when someone was picking me up. My apartment was upstairs; I didn't mind that, at least I wouldn't hear people walking over my head.

Junior seemed happy to be in his room; he had toys to play with. The girl who lived downstairs had a son, too. He was about the same age as Junior and in a cast. She lived with her baby's father. They were a family, which is what I wanted for Junior and me.

Junior would occasionally look out of his window, crying that he didn't have anyone to play with and wanted a brother or a sister. I think it was because he would see Carol and her son, the girl who lived downstairs when they would go in and out of the building.

Carol and I became friends. After her son was out of the cast, he and Junior would play together.

Carol's apartment was decorated nicely. Her walls had printed wallpaper on them, the living room walls was done with aluminum foil, and she had one of those lights that was in the club that made your clothes look like lint was on them. The speakers to her stereo were on the walls. Every time she played her music, my floor would vibrate. She also had a floor-model color TV. I know she was on welfare like me, but her boyfriend worked. So, she was able to have a lot of nice things that I couldn't afford.

When my first welfare check came, a letter came after it stating that it was the wrong amount. I still cashed it; my friend worked at the bank. I wanted a floor model color TV and some new living room furniture. So, I went to this place downtown called The Furniture Store and got a floor-model TV, a brown living room set, and a coffee table. They allowed me to pay on the first and sixteenth when I got my welfare check until I paid it off.

The time came for my next check, and the rent was due, but no check came. I called the welfare office to inquire. They told me my worker was on vacation, and they saw where she had sent me a check. I told them I didn't get it. They told me I must file a police report stating the check was stolen.

After I hung up the phone, all I could think about was I was going to have to go back to my mother's house. They would see I signed and cashed the check and know I lied. I'm done. I just said, "Oh God, what will I do?" Then I heard, "Call them back and tell them you lied."

After pacing my bedroom for a while, I called them back and said, "I lied." the woman on the other end of the phone said she would need to speak to her supervisor and would call me back, then hung up, slamming the phone down. I was so afraid of having to go back to my mother's all because I wanted a floor model color TV like Carol downstairs.

The worker didn't call me back. I called her back just before the office closed. She said in a stern and disgusted voice that you will be receiving another check and do what you are supposed to do with it. I was happy to hear those words. She could have cussed me out, called me anything she wanted to as long as I was getting another check and not going back to my mother's house. I didn't care how she treated me; I was wrong.

I learned my first adult lesson: don't play with your money for the roof over your head. And don't try to be like anyone else. When the check came, I immediately went to the rental office and paid my rent. I was also able to get a phone installed in my apartment. So, I wouldn't have to go to Zion's mother's house when he called. I wrote to him and told him I had a new apartment and my phone, and now he could call directly to me.

I hadn't heard from Zion for a while, but he told me that it might be because of training and duty. I missed him and us being together, especially when I would see Carol with her baby's father. I enjoyed my apartment; there was always a party on the first and sixteenth of the month. I had to get my nickel or dime bag of weed, wine coolers, and munchies, but I paid rent and phone bill before anything.

At the beginning of our friendship, Zion's sister Reesie would come over from time to time. I think she was spying for her brother, ensuring I wasn't doing anyone else. When you have a baby young, or shall I say when people know you are having sex, they look at you differently. I wasn't anything like what they thought.

I enjoyed her company; we got along very well, maybe because we were both teenagers. Reesie had a wild side to her; she was free-spirited, but I liked her. We became good friends. Reesie started to spend a lot of time at my apartment doing what we do: smoking weed, dancing, eating, and singing some of our favorite songs. She was a church girl, the youngest of Zion's siblings. They were close.

When Zion came home from basic training, my apartment was the first place he came to. When he knocked on the door, I wasn't prepared at all; Junior and I had just been lying around watching TV. We hadn't put on clothes for the day. I wasn't expecting anyone and had no plans of going anywhere.

The knock on the door kind of scared us. I went to the door and peeped out the peephole; the person standing in the hall had their back turned so I couldn't see their face. Because of the starch white Navy uniform, I knew it was Zion. I didn't open the door right away; I wasn't dressed right, Junior's toys were all over the living room, and my hair wasn't combed. Junior didn't know what was going on. All he was doing was sitting on the floor, watching me run around, trying to pick up and get dressed.

Zion knocked again; my heart was racing; I knew I had to open the door. I wanted to open the door. I knew I couldn't leave him in the hall until I cleaned up and dressed completely. I opened the door. His face was facing me. He looked so fine in that uniform. I could see his masculine form, his muscles slightly bulging from the inside of his uniform. The Navy had made him even more handsome.

He was not the same Zion that left, body-wise. When he grabbed me and hugged me, I could feel his muscles; they were hard as rocks, and his chest was full and solid. He hugged me so tight I could feel the release of what he had experienced for the past eight weeks leave his body.

He kissed me for the longest time. Then he grabbed Junior, standing next to me, picked him up, and hugged and kissed him on his forehead. He was so happy to see us; he didn't notice how we looked.

I noticed he had his duffle bag with him; I asked him if I was the first place He came. He said, "Yes, I was the first face he wanted to see when he came home." I showed him around the apartment, and he said he liked it.

We sat for a while, then he said he was going to go home but would be back later, and he asked if I could get someone to watch Junior because he had plans for us, and you could really get dressed.

I walked him to the door, we kissed, and he whispered in my ear, "I've been waiting for you." I knew what that meant; I just said, "Me too."

Later that night, when Zion came back, he didn't have his uniform on, and he still looked fine in his fitted jeans and silk shirt, and he smelled good, too. I cleaned up the apartment, and Junior was with my mother. Zion had brought some wine coolers and weed. We sat in the living room listening to music.

I wanted to touch his bare chest. His arms felt strong and hard. As we began to caress each other's bodies, all I could think of was Zion was home. I'm feeling something I never felt for him before. I want to give him some. I never wanted to have sex like I wanted to now.

He felt so good. He grabbed my hand, picked me up, and took me to the bedroom; he told me to lay still and close my eyes; he undressed me slowly as he kissed my body, and then I felt a light feather gently moving over my body. Every time it crossed my breast, I felt a chill to my core, and my toes tingled.

I was so high I just lost myself in the moment; I let him do whatever he wanted to. I think I love him. Zion began kissing my body all over. As he kissed me, I couldn't lay still anymore. I began rubbing my hands all over his beautiful body, touching and squeezing every muscle.

"Raelynn, what are you doing?" I thought. Never had I been this free, and I wanted him. As I opened to him, it happened: pain and pleasure all at the same time.

After we lay in the bed smoking a cigarette and drinking another wine cooler, he said, "You are so beautiful." We talked about our future together. I felt guilt, shame, pain, and pleasure all at the same time. I loved this man; I believe that was what I was feeling.

Zion stayed that night. The next morning, before he left, he told me to be ready later because he wanted to take Junior and me shopping. I didn't want him to leave, but I knew we couldn't stay together forever. I'm sure his mother wanted to spend time with him. He is only home for two weeks, then off to his assigned naval base. We saw each other every day he was home; he spent most of his time with us.

The two weeks flew by; it was time for Zion to leave, and my heart sank. He said he would hold out until we see each other again and asked me to wait. I had my mind set on waiting for him. There was no one else for me and Junior. I walked him down the stairs. He looked so good in his uniform; I watched him walk down the street toward his house.

Zion and I wrote to each other daily so that we would each get a letter once a week if not more. In one of his letters, he told me that the ship was going out on a six-month cruise, and the letters may be a little slow coming. I read his letters repeatedly until a new one came.

He would tell me of some places they would go and about some of the guys on the ship. It was as if I was there. In one of his letters, he asked me to marry him when he left the Navy. I replied, "Ask me again when you come home."

To pass the time, I would do things with the younger children in the neighborhood, including my brothers and sisters. I still hung out at Ms. Millie's house, chilling with Reesie and going to the club with Carol. I would do almost anything to pass the time.

Christmas was coming, and I got the usual call that my father had sent me something. For some reason, I wasn't as excited about receiving the gifts. He wasn't there. I can't talk to and tell him about what's going on in my life. I can't see his bright smile and the gold shining from his teeth. I wonder what it would feel like to have him to hold me and my head lay on his shoulders as he tells me what a father tells his little girl he adores.

I wanted to tell him I think I'm in love. I want him to meet the one I love. I want him to walk me down the aisle when and if I get married. He consistently remembered birthdays and Christmas; at least, I know he was thinking about me. Somehow, my mother always knew when Titus would send me a gift. I think my aunt would tell her because I'm sure she and Titus were not talking to one another.

It was my first Christmas in my apartment. Junior and I were putting up our tree. I bought him some toys and new clothes for Christmas. Now that he is older, he understands it a little more. I don't remember what Junior had done as we were putting the tree up, but whatever it was, I was upset and told him to go to his room before I beat his ass.

He went to his room, and a few minutes later, he came out with big tears in his eye and said Mommy "please don't beat my ass." Oh my God, he is saying what I say. I don't want him to cuss, drink, or smoke, another adult lesson learned. If I don't want him to do it, don't do it in front of him, and don't say it. He was beginning to do and say what I do. I was his mommy, and he looked up to me for everything, even how to be when he grew up.

I grabbed him, hugged him, and said, "I'm not going to beat your ass, and don't say that word no more." His face would always melt my heart.

The family had dinner at my aunt's house the day after Christmas. She gave me a gift from my father; it was always money. He didn't know what I wanted, so money would be safest. That way, I could buy whatever I wanted or needed. I rarely spent the money on myself; I would always buy Junior something, but because New Year's was approaching, a bag of weed.

We had a ball on New Year's Eve. Junior was at my mother's; I invited some friends from the neighborhood over for a get-high party; the music was playing, and Carol's speaker was vibrating the wall. We would bring this year in feeling nice, and we did.

Carol's music didn't bother me, and my noise over her didn't bother her; our side of the building was celebrating the new year.

New Year's morning, we woke up to a pile of snow it looked like old man winter had partied too. I hated the snow and the cold. Every time a big snowfall came, I went into a funk. I didn't go outside for days. I had my sister bring Junior home once the snow stopped. It was a blizzard for days, Happy New Year to us from old man winter.

As the days and months passed and the weather began to change, Carol and I would shop for new outfits to go to the club on Friday and Saturday and sleep in on Sunday. We would get to the club late when we knew most of the people were already there. We wanted to make a grand entrance because we knew everybody saw everybody in their outfits. So, when we came in, all eyes were on us.

One Saturday night, while getting dressed, I took a tab of mescaline and put it in my gum so it would dissolve slowly; by the time I got to the club, I would feel nice. Carol and I walked to the club that night and smoked a joint before we left home. We didn't like our clothes smelling like weed. The club was just over the bridge from our apartments.

Once we got to the club, Carol's favorite song was playing, and she went right to the dance floor. I found a table and sat down. The music seemed to be louder than usual, and the people in the club looked different. They looked disfigured and distorted. Then I realized the mescaline was taking effect. This is going to be a good trip. I'm feeling nice.

I sat there looking around, my head and body swaying to the music. I heard someone say, "What are you doing here?" I looked around and no one was near me. I continued to chair dance, and then I heard the voice again but louder, "What are you doing here?" Look around," the voice said, "Look at him, look at her. They're doing the same old things with different people. Go home!"

I knew I was tripping. When Carol came to the table, I told her I was going home. She wasn't happy about that because we had just got there. I didn't tell her about the mescaline; I knew I had to go home. When I stepped outside the club, a car was parked in front with a man sitting in it.

New Birth

He looked at me and asked, "If I needed a ride, " I said, "Yes." He opened the door and asked, "Where are you going?" I told him I was going home. Within minutes, I was at my front door, going up the stairs and into my apartment.

When I walked into my apartment, the same voice that I now knew, was in my head said, "Get your bible." At first, I didn't remember I had a bible, but I instantly went to it in my living room. It was inside the end table under a bunch of stuff.

I opened the book and found myself in the book of Revelation, chapter nine, and my eyes focused on the words that read. "The locusts looked like horses prepared for battle. On their heads, they wore something like crowns of gold, and their faces resembled human faces. Their hair was like women's hair, and their teeth were like loin's teeth. They had breastplates like breastplates of iron, and the sound of their wings was like the thundering of many horses and chariots rushing into battle. They had tails with stingers like scorpions, and in their tails, they had the power to torment people for five months."

Just as I finished reading then, I turned the pages again to another part of the Book of Revelation and read, "The unbelieving, the vile, the murderers, the fornicators, and all liars shall have their part in the lake of fire."

Suddenly, my living room was filled with locusts, and their tails were trying to sting me. I was screaming and trying to fight them off, but they kept coming more and more.

I screamed, "God, please help me!" the voice said, "Go, look at yourself."

I went to my bathroom. While fighting off the creatures, I closed the bathroom door, looked at myself eye to eye in the mirror, and flames of fire shot out of my eyes. I screamed and fell to my bathroom floor; I began to pray, "God, please forgive me. I'm a liar and an unbeliever; I'm sorry; please forgive me and help me."

I lay on my bathroom floor crying. It seemed like hours when I opened my bathroom door and saw clouds everywhere but no locusts. I had a peace I had never felt before, but the voice was still there, and He said, "Get your bible."

I picked my bible up from the floor where I had dropped it and opened to the Book of Revelation again, this time reading chapter two and read, "and I heard a voice from the throne saying Look! God's dwelling place is now among the people, and God himself will be with them, and they will be his people, and he will be their God. He will wipe every tear from their eyes. There will be no more death, mourning, crying, or pain, for the old order of things has passed away. He, who was seated on the throne, said, "I am making everything new!" I closed the bible, and I knew I had changed.

I felt new. I felt free in my being. I knew now the voice I was hearing was His voice. He said, "You hated your mother, but you were really hating me." I wanted to go to my mother and grab her, hug her, and tell her that I was sorry for everything I had ever said or done to hurt her. I did just that. The next morning, on my way to the same church my aunt and Uncle took me to when I lived with them. I now have love in my heart, a real love; I knew it was love.

When I knocked on the door to my mother's house, she opened it. I stood there for a moment, wanting to hug her, but her face said don't, so I told her I was sorry and love you. She just looked at me with a look of shock and said whatever, "Why are you so sorry now? You weren't sorry when you said and did what you did? I said, "I'm sorry now." She said, "Ok," and closed the door.

Once I got to church, I sat down on the front row until one of the ladies dressed in white told me it was the mother's seat, so I moved to the second row. My heart would jump whenever they sang about God or Jesus. I was on my feet before I knew it with my hands raised in the air.

I don't know what the pastor preached about that Sunday. All I was waiting for was the altar call. When the altar call was made, I was the first one there; I told the church I was making an open confession to my belief in and love for God.

I received the right hand of fellowship and became a candidate for baptism. My Uncle seconded the motion. He was surprised and proud. My aunt was shocked to see me go to the altar because she and some of the other family members thought I would wind up in the streets or a drug addict. My life was headed that way.

At that moment, I didn't care; I had been given real love. I loved Him more than my son. God has forgiven me for everything. I won't be a part of those in the lake of fire. He was in my soul and on my mind all the time. I had a new found joy and peace.

When I got home, Carol came upstairs and asked why I left the club so early. I told her everything. I told her I was saved now, and God blew my high. I was so excited, and she said I looked different. I told her I was different. She said she wasn't ready to attend church but was happy for me.

Then she asked if I wanted to fire up one. I had no desire to get high anymore; it wasn't about that for me anymore. I didn't want to do anything that would hurt the new lover of my soul. I knew beyond a shadow of any doubt that He loved me. She said, "Ok, it's good." I said, "I'm good!" As she was about to light the joint, I said, "Not in here anymore." She left and went to her apartment.

The next day, I got a letter from Zion with a joint in it. He said he got the weed from overseas, and it was good. I broke it up and flushed it in the toilet. I am not the same person he left. So, I wrote to him and told him I was saved and didn't do what I used to do. Once I found out what fornication meant, I told him I would not be sleeping with him anymore.

The letter I received after telling him I was saved didn't have the same tone as all the others. He said he would return to base soon and then home for about three weeks. I was excited to read those words but was afraid of how I would react to seeing him after receiving my new life.

I read the bible more than I read Zion's letters. I wanted to know all I could about my savior. I went to bible study on Wednesday, Sunday school, and afternoon service on Sunday. The older women at church would comment on how good Junior was and how he would sit still and be quiet throughout the service. They didn't know we had the talk before we got to the church. He knew to go to the potty before church started. I had a book and crayons to keep him busy. Sometimes, he had nothing and just sat there.

The neighborhood people also commented on how they would see Junior and me cutting across the field going to the church and how I would have Junior dressed in his little suits and look like a little man. Some would let Junior Walk into their house, go into their refrigerator, and get whatever he wanted.

Everyone could see the change. When they would ask me what happened, I would tell them. My life changes spoke so loudly my mouth didn't have to say a word.

Some people said it wasn't going to last. They had to see and read what I read; if hell was in me, God scared the hell out of me that night.

I watched all the televangelist shows; my favorite was Oral Roberts. Junior knew exactly when it came on. He would tell me Ma, something good is coming on. He knew the words to the theme song. I also watched Kenneth Hagin and Kathryn Kuhlman. I wanted to hear everyone I thought could tell me about the one I loved. Junior would watch with me, liking Hanna Barbera's Christian cartoons. Junior and I would also pray together.

Junior had frequent ear infections and was scheduled for surgery. The night before, he and I kneeled by his bed; and prayed for God to heal him. He remembered Oral Roberts and said what he said: "Be healed in Jesus' name."

The next day, I got him to the hospital by seven a.m. as they asked me to. The surgeon came in and asked many questions; the nurse gave him a shot to relax him before the surgery.

The surgeon looked inside Junior's ears again and asked me how his hearing was; I told him it was good because he was tested a week ago. The doctor looked in his ears again and said, "I can't find anything wrong with him; you can take him home. He will probably sleep for the rest of the day because of the shot."

I went to my knees right there, lifted my hands, and said, "Thank You, Jesus!" The doctor and the nurse looked at me and walked out. I grabbed Junior, got him dressed, and caught the bus home from the hospital. He slept all day and through the night. Junior was healed. Oral Roberts was right; there is power in the name of Jesus.

My mother wanted to know how the surgery went. I told her Jesus healed him, and he didn't have to have it. She looked at me and said, "Ok, if you say so." I could tell she didn't believe me. I knew she loved Junior and would do anything for him.

I remember she almost fought a lady three doors down from us when we lived with her because the lady told her son to hit Junior with a stick. I never saw my mother that upset and wanting to fight. The lady ran into the house and would not come out. She didn't let her son come out to play for days. My mother may not have believed me, but she cared about her grandson's well-being.

It was getting close to the time for Zion to come home; his sister Reesie came over and told me he would be home that Friday. She wanted to smoke. I told her I don't do that anymore; she said nothing. I said nothing. I don't want to; I told her I was saved now and didn't know how Zion would take it. She just shrugged her shoulders and shook her head as if to say I don't know.

She said she's been in church all her life and is not ready for all that stuff. I knew that because Zion told me the church they were going to had started in his mother's living room. Now that I know the Lord, He speaks to me. I wondered how they could do the things they did. How can they hurt Him like that and love Him, too? How could they be in church all their lives and not fear being a part of the lake of fire? I didn't share those thoughts with her; I just wondered.

On Friday morning, I had gotten up early, cleaned the apartment, and made sure I got dressed early because I didn't know what time Zion was coming. Just when I finished everything and was about to sit down, there was a knock on the door. I looked out the peephole, and there he stood with his white sailor hat on, a blue pea coat, his whites with shining black shoes, and his duffle bag. He came here first, again.

My heartbeat was so fast I just prayed before I opened the door: Lord, please help me; I love you. Then I opened the door. He came in and put his duffle bag down. We hugged and kissed, but not tongue-kissed. I wouldn't let him do that. I told him the letter was true. I'm not the same.

He said OK, then he began to open his duffle and poured out all these drugs on the table. Thank God Junior wasn't there; I told him I don't do that anymore, and he couldn't do it here either. He said OKAY and told me to get closer to him. He was holding me and told me he had been waiting for me. He said he hadn't slept with anyone even though at some of the ports, women were there waiting for the sailors. He said he was faithful and beat himself into submission.

My body went into instant recall of the feeling I felt before he left when we would have sex. I also had a flashback of the words I read in Revelation: "Fornicators shall have their place in the Lake of Fire."

He kept saying he loved me. I told him, I love him, and I'm not going to hell for my son, so I know I'm not going for you.

If you truly love me, you will marry me. He said he was going to, but not now. When he leaves the Navy, he could be a better provider for us. I said, "Ok, but we can't sleep together until then." He got upset, grabbed his stuff, and left.

When the door slammed, I hurt so bad I just cried. "God," I said, I give him up for you. If he is not the one, I know you have someone else better for me." There goes my having a father for my son and a family to call mine. I thought I had Zion, who promised He would never leave me. After a while, God gave me peace. I felt it was going to be okay.

Zion would still come around the neighborhood; he would go to visit Ms. Millie's. She would tell me he would come crying to her. He didn't understand why I didn't want to be with him. Ms. Millie knew about my life change and told him I was for real. Everybody in the village we knew told him. I asked Ms. Millie to let me know when he was coming again because I had a set of dog tags, he had given me, and I wanted to return them.

I was walking around the corner toward my mother's apartment when I saw Zion coming toward me. I stopped him, and we sat on the steps. I took off the dog tags and gave them to him. He said he didn't want them because they were only dog tags in a degrading way. I told him as I walked away and put them on the step. I hope one of your dog's comes and finds them. I was done, free, and at peace.

During the last week of Zion's leave, he came over. I didn't let him in right away; we stood at the door, and I didn't talk; I just listened. He said he was sorry for what he said about the dog tags; he was hurt. Then he said he couldn't live without me and to please let him back in. I let him come in, and we sat in the living room; just as I sat down, he got on one knee, grabbed my hand, and said, "Raelynn, I can't live without you. Will you marry me and set a date?" I knew he was for real. I could see it in his eyes.

I was so happy I said, "Yes," he pulled me up from the couch, picked me up off my feet, hugged me so tight, and kissed me. I still didn't tongue-kiss him because I knew it would start something. He said before he left, we would shop for rings. I told him I didn't need an engagement ring; I wanted a wedding band. We didn't have time for engagement.

Zion and I were back together again. I said, "God, thank you. You love me, and you know I love you, too. Our relationship is more important to me than any other one; you know I want to live right before you. You sent him back."

The night before Zion had to leave for the ship, he came over. I didn't want him to go back; I wanted to marry him before he left. He told me again to set the date, and he would make sure he put in for the leave. He said the ship would be going back out in August, so it can't be in that month.

He told me about his mother's response to him asking me to marry him. Her response was the same as before; She told him he would have a ready-made family and why he didn't like any girls at the church.

Zion said he told her he was in love with me and would marry me. I didn't know that when we got married, I would receive an allotment. I asked Zion again if he was sure because his mother was right.

He said he wanted to live the rest of his life with me and wanted us to grow old together. This is what I wanted, too. I didn't want to be like my mother, going from man to man, nor other family members, to see me with a lot of different men. I knew Junior didn't know his father; he knew of him but didn't spend much time with him.

I asked Junior's father once to help me get some clothes off layaway, and he told me to let that nigga you with get them for you. I told him, I will never ask you again for a dime. I will never talk bad about you to your son or stop you from seeing him. When he gets older, he will learn you for himself, and I want him to know you.

Zion had brought a cassette over he wanted me to hear by Heatwave. He put it on and began to sing "Always and Forever"; he had a beautiful voice. I began to melt. He sang it with true sincerity; I knew he meant every word.

When the song ended, I kissed him and allowed him to tongue-kiss me. I began to feel hot all over my body; my body was screaming, and I wanted to feel his caress. He didn't know what to do or think. I could tell by how he responded to me, allowing him to French kiss me.

I could tell my body wanted him; I wanted him. We began to caress each other, touching forbidden areas. "God, what am I doing?" I have gone too far, now at the point of no return. I wanted to scream, "No, Stop!" But it wouldn't come out, only moans and groans; it was as if an invisible hand was over my mouth. I screamed once I felt him inside of me. It felt so good, but my spirit felt horrible.

When we were done, I just cried, "I hurt Him; I hurt the lover of my soul. Everything within me felt pain; oh God! Oh God, please, please forgive me." I rolled out of bed onto the floor, crying and praying. Zion said, "I'm so sorry; I shouldn't have done that." He tried to comfort me by assuring me he would marry me. He didn't understand.

But I can't blame it all on him; I wanted it, too. Lesson learned: I shouldn't allow myself to be put in the position again; I should always be in a crowd. Junior should have been home. We lay there until morning, when he had to leave. As he got ready to leave, he could tell I wasn't myself, and I could see he wasn't happy about how he was leaving me. I love him too, which I told him as we kissed before he walked out the door.

After he left, I took the sheets off the bed, put them in the wash, and took a shower. Then, I got on my knees again and prayed, "God, please don't leave me. I am so sorry; I can't believe I did that. Forgive me, Lord. I promise that won't happen again until I am married."

Then I opened my bible and read the first thing I saw in Matthew 28:2: "I will be with you always, even until the end of the world." I praised God. I knew He heard me and forgave me. I loved him even more. I promised myself that it would never happen again. I don't want to ever feel like He left or abandoned me.

I had to pick a date to marry Zion; it was still cold out, so I wanted a summer or spring wedding. I looked at the calendar and knew it had to be before August and after April.

So, I picked June. I was still seventeen; I couldn't get married at seventeen. My mother would have to sign for me.

A few days after Zion left, I talked to my mother, told her we wanted to get married, and asked if she would sign for me because I wasn't old enough. She said she would. She was kind of happy for me and that she was going to plan a wedding. I told her that I planned for June 24th of the coming year.

I asked Uncle D if he would give me away, and he said he would. My auntie said we could have the wedding at her house; the wedding will be in the front yard and the reception in the back yard.

When Zion called, I told him the date, and he agreed. I told him we would keep it small. Man will be the ring-bearer, little Kenya will be my flower girl, and my cousin Aneesa will be my Maid of Honor. He said he would have his brother Neal as his best man.

After the date was set and plans being put into place time seemed to fly by. I only had one major thing to buy: my dress. I found it in the bridal department at Sibley's on sale for $19.99. It fits perfectly. I didn't have to have any alterations; it was as if the dress was waiting for me.

Zion came home three days before the wedding. The day before the wedding, he and the guys stayed at my apartment, and Junior stayed with them. I stayed at my aunt's house. Uncle D had become sick and could not walk me down the front steps, so Uncle Red stepped in. Most of my family members who lived in New York were there, and I was happy my Grand-ma-ma was there, too.

Zion's mother, Reesie, and his younger brother, Manny, were there. The new youth pastor from the church married us. Junior wouldn't come down the stairs; he came out the door and then turned around. It's good that he didn't have the rings; Zion's brother did.

The day was nice; Zion and I were married. We left the next day for our honeymoon. We went to Niagara Falls, Canada. The people in Canada couldn't believe we were married; they thought we were brother and sister. We told them we were on our honeymoon. We stayed at the Foxhead Hotel overlooking the falls.

The first night was beautiful, but there was a difference after we consummated our marriage. It felt clean, it felt pure. I felt no soul pain or a feeling of horror. I felt like God had blessed us. I came to love being with Zion; he knew how to make me feel special, loved, and wanted.

I am a wife now. After the honeymoon, Zion had to leave to return to the ship. He told me everything to expect in the mail from the Navy now that we're married. I wasn't going to see him for months.

When I got my first allotment, I opened a bank account for us. I also wrote a letter to the welfare office, thanking them for their assistance, but I no longer needed it. They sent me a letter with a check for three hundred dollars and seventy-four cents, closing my case.

My life was changed again. We are a family: Zion, me, and Junior. I thanked God for our little family every day. When I would go to church and, I'd hear them sing any song about Jesus, especially "What a Friend We Have in Jesus." I would stand up, lift my hands, and praise God so loud. I started to notice I was the only one doing it.

When I went to Aunt V's, Uncle D teased me by saying, "Gal, you get happy every devilish Sunday." I asked him, "Don't you? Jesus saved you, too. Aren't you happy about it?" He would just laugh and tell me to read the bible for myself and don't believe everything the devilish preachers tell me.

I told Zion that the church I was going to didn't praise God like I did, and I felt out of place. He said I should go with his mother one Sunday. So, I called Mama, Zion's mother, and asked if she would pick me and Junior up for church the next Sunday.

Sunday came, and we were ready when she pulled up in front of the door. Once the service started, they started singing, and drums, piano, and tambourine were playing. I saw hands go up and mouths open, praising the Lord, and before I knew it, I was doing the same. I felt at home.

That Monday, I called the church I was going to with my aunt and Uncle and asked if I could meet with the pastor. At the meeting, I told them I was led to leave and paid up my church dues. I thanked them for everything I had learned while there. I received the pastor's blessing and began attending church with Zion's mother.

They believed strongly in God's Word and trusted God for their healing. They were like a big family of families. I joined the church, and they openly welcomed me and Junior.

As time passed, most of my time was spent at church and with Zion's family. I loved his mother and wished my mother was more like her. She was a woman who loved the Lord, took her children to church, and could sing and pray like I never heard before. She loved wearing hats, and she bought me my first hat from this fancy hat store called Kipling's, which is near Midtown, downtown. She said I had the perfect face for hats.

I enjoyed shopping with her and my sisters in love. Even though I had a phone, and Zion would call sometimes when the ship was in port, I wrote him letters once a week telling him about the time I was spending with his family.

It has been about a month or so since the honeymoon and I didn't get my period. In the letter to Zion, I told him I think I am pregnant. It turned out I was pregnant. So, I told him in the next letter. He called me when he got the letter, he was very happy. When I told Junior he would have a little brother or a sister, he was happy, too.

Zion wanted to know when the baby was due. The doctor said March. He told me his father's birthday was in March, and maybe the baby would come around his birthday. His father had died when he was 12. He looked just like him.

I would talk to the baby every day, especially at night, while lying in bed. For some reason, I knew it was a girl. As my stomach grew, and the baby began to move it seemed as if she would communicate with each movement. I was having a baby, this time the right way, married, knowing the man loved me.

My Grand-ma-ma called to tell me my father brought something to her house for my birthday. She was sorry she was late getting it to me. While talking to her, I heard a knock on the door. I hung up with my Grand-ma-ma to answer it.

When I looked out the peephole, this person stood with their back turned so I couldn't see their face. I said, "Who is it?" It was a man, but it wasn't Zion; this guy was too tall to be Zion. From the back, I couldn't tell who it was. I asked again who it was. I won't open the door until you turn around so I can see who you are.

Just as they turned around, they put their finger over the peephole. I said stop playing; I'm not letting you in until I see who you are. I looked again through the peephole, and to my surprise, I could believe my eyes, my heart dropped to the pit of my stomach. It was Praxton; it was really Praxton standing in the hall, knocking on my door. Oh my God, it was Praxton.

I opened the door, he said hi, I said hi, he leaned in and kissed me on the cheek, he asked if he could come in from the hallway. We sat down at the dining room table. He told me I looked good. He said I told you I was coming back for you.

I asked him how he knew where I lived. He said he went to my mother's, and she told him. He saw the wedding band on my finger as he looked at me. I noticed his facial expression changed.

I said, "Yes, I'm married now and saved. I'm sure you noticed that I'm pregnant too." I told him after not hearing from him, I didn't think you were coming back, and you had a girlfriend, and your family wanted you to marry. What was I supposed to think?

He looked at me as if he would cry, then asked me if I was happy. Was the guy treating me well? I said yes and yes. He said then I'm happy for you. If you are happy, but I don't want you to forget if you need anything, let me know. I will always care for you. We began to talk about some things that were going on in his life, and he said he and the girl had broken up. She was a gold digger. The family initially didn't see it, but her true colors came out.

I shared with him that I was talking to my Grand-ma-ma just before he came because she had a gift from my father, who I don't know; he sent me gifts for my birthday and Christmas. I don't know why we can't have a real father-daughter relationship. Why can't I get to know my other brothers and sisters?

Praxton asked if I had ever just called and asked him. He said if you want to know you should call him. Wow, a light went off when he said, "Just call him." I knew it was time I was older now and had children, and I wanted them to know their grandfather.

Praxton said he would stay in town for a while, helping his older brother out with his company. As we walked to the door, he asked if he could hug me, and I agreed. We hugged, he kissed me on the cheek, looked into my eyes, and said, "Remember what I said. And take care of yourself and those babies. He is a lucky man." Then he walked out the door and down the stairs. After all those years, God knew I needed that closure.

Sharmeka Lee

I felt a sense of peace and closure when I closed the door. There were times I would wonder what happened to him. I thank God now I know.

Time passed so fast that my due date was approaching. I wanted Zion to be home for the birth of our baby. My doctor sent a letter to his commanding officer but to no avail. He said it wasn't a serious enough matter for a sailor to leave the ship off a cruise out at sea. I didn't care what the commander said, I felt he would be home.

I also felt so strongly that I was having a girl. I started calling her by the name I would give her, "Sharmeka Lee," the beginning of my name and Zion's middle name.

I would shop with my mother but never buy anything for the baby. My auntie gave me a baby shower. I got a housecoat, slippers, bath towels, tee shirts and diapers. Someone gave me some little girl hand-me-downs. Knowing she was coming; I didn't know why I hadn't bought anything to prepare for her.

The morning, I went into labor, I was home, and I couldn't stop peeing; my sister-in-love Reesie was there. She said, "Your water broke," and got a towel for me to put between my legs, using my panties to hold it up. I called my auntie who came to take me to the hospital.

Once at the hospital and in the labor room, I began to feel the pain start; they had me lay in the bed with a baby monitor strapped around my stomach. I wanted to walk. Every time I felt pain, my aunt would say, try to relax so your muscles won't tighten because that will make it harder for the baby to come through.

As the pain got stronger and lasted longer. I told my aunt I wanted to choke Eve. She asked," Who is Eve?" Eve, Adam's wife, if it wasn't for her, we wouldn't have been in this much pain. She just looked at me as if to say, ok!

The doctor came in to check on me because I felt like I had to use the bathroom, but when he checked me, he said no! I can see the baby's head. It's time to push. They wheeled me into the delivery room and pushed I did!

Sharmeka was here! Crying, red and beautiful to me, after they cleaned her up the nurse laid her in my arms. She instantly stopped crying. I looked at her and said, "Hi, we finally met," her eyes were opened wide. She had all her fingers and toes, but she had Zion's nose and lips. I told her I was sorry; I slept with your daddy and smiled.

She didn't take her eyes off me even when I told her to go to sleep because I was tired, and I knew she was too. As I would drift off to sleep with her still in my arms, each time I would open my eyes she would be looking at me. I thought it was a little strange but dismissed the thought.

My aunt came in to see me and the baby after they put us back in the labor room, and then she left. My mother was working at the hospital and came in later. When the room in the maternity ward was ready, the nurse from the nursery took the baby so they could clean her more and check her over. She told me she would bring her later so I could feed her.

Later that evening, the nurse that was assigned to Sharmeka brought her in for me to feed her. She had her blankets wrapped tight around her, the nurse told me to keep her wrapped because they were trying to get her temperature regulated. My roommate's husband was taking pictures of her and their little boy and asked if I wanted a picture of me and Sharmeka. I told him I would love it. I thought I could send it to Zion.

As he was taking the picture, I told Sharmeka to look at the camera, and she turned her head and looked at my roommate's husband and we was like wow. He took the picture from the Polaroid camera and gave it to me. When it dried, I looked at the picture, and Sharmeka looked up at me.

She did not suck her bottle. When the nurse came to get her, I told her she didn't drink much. She said it takes a little time for some babies. She said she would bring her back in the morning.

The next day, while waiting for the nurse to bring Sharmeka back, a lady came into my room, said," Hello," introduced herself, and began talking to me about her baby and how her baby was having difficulty when he was firstborn. I thought, "Why is this lady in my room talking to me about this?" As she left, she said, "I'll be praying." I just said, "Ok, thank you."

It started to be late morning, and the nurse hadn't brought Sharmeka yet, so I walked down to the nursery. I saw her little basinet with our last name written on it, but she wasn't there. I returned to my room, and my doctor awaited me.

I could tell from the look on his face something wasn't right. He said, "Raelynn, your baby is very sick, she is fighting off your blood, and they can't get her heart rate regulated." He asked me if I wanted him to call someone; he also said he would talk to the hospital social worker to contact the Red Cross to inform my husband about what was happening. I told him my family would be up later and my mother worked here.

After my doctor left, I got on my knees and began to pray, "God, I know now that you have the power of life and death. I pray you help Zion wherever he may be now when he gets the news that his baby girl is very sick. I put us in your hands." My heart and soul ached with new pain; it was as if my spirit was torn, a rip that could not be mended.

By the time I was done praying and had just gotten back into bed, one of the doctors from the nursery who was taking care of Sharmeka came in with my doctor. He told me that she was not going to make it; he said, "Your baby is dying. We have done all that we can. We want you to come hold her and say your goodbyes." While they were still talking to me, my sister-in-love Reesie entered the room. My doctor said a nurse would be able to take me to her.

When I got to Sharmeka, the doctors and the nurses were still in the room with her, and one of them put her in my arms. I held her tight; her eyes were closed. She didn't look at me anymore. I looked at her this time, knowing it would be the last. I told her I love her, and I promise you I will see you again.

I'm so sorry your father didn't get the chance to see those beautiful eyes. Then I kissed her and said, "I will see you again." I felt no more life in her; her breath was no longer. I gave her little body back to the nurse. My sister-in-love and I returned to my room, now a private room, with no roommate and her baby.

Reesie said she was going to call her mother. I was numb, my baby. My mind had so many thoughts racing in it. One loud thought was, "This is payback for the abortion. I hope you know God is truly in control of life and death." I realized that more now than ever. I knew I couldn't let that thought take me to a dark place. God has forgiven me, and I knew it. My mind then went to Junior. How am I going to tell him he won't have his playmate?

By that evening, my room was full, Zion's mother and most of the people from the church. I was grateful, but Zion wasn't there, or my mother, to put their arms around me and tell me you're going to be okay. It was Zion's mother there.

My father was not there to rub my head, kiss my forehead, and tell me I love you, I'm proud of you, and you will make it through this. But He was there, the lover of my soul; I felt His presence so strong during all the pain I felt.

I was discharged from the hospital the next day, but before they asked me what I wanted to do with Sharmeka's body. They said they could dispose of it. My mother-in-law spoke up and said we would have the funeral home come and get her.

When I got to my apartment, my mother was there with Junior, my sisters, and my brother. I took Junior into his room to tell him about his sister. I said Junior, she was so beautiful and bright-eyed. God brought her back to him, and he will send you another brother or sister to play with. I showed him her picture. He said, "Ok, mommy." Then he asked if he could return to the living room with everybody. That was easier than I thought it would be.

I just wanted to be alone, but people kept coming over. I wanted Zion home; I stayed in my room most of the time, and my body was doing what it does after having a baby. My breasts filled with milk, my arms longing to hold my baby, my womb contracting back into place, empty.

My mother-in-love kept trying to get me to eat. She told me if I didn't, I would get sick, and I needed to be healthy for my family. Food wasn't going to fill the emptiness I was feeling.

I thought about Zion, and how he would be when he got home, so I ate a little because I didn't want to be sick when he came home. The Red Cross had gotten in touch with the ship, and they were flying him home from overseas. I knew he was coming home I just didn't know it would be for our baby's funeral.

It seemed like time was standing still; days were taking so long, even though only four days had passed. Zion will be home tomorrow. I was thankful for my mother taking care of Junior. I was in a daze.

There was always someone in my apartment. They would not leave me alone. I wanted to be alone, but I was happy someone was there. Most were from the church. I was getting phone calls from family members down south saying how sorry they were to hear the news of my baby. No call from my father.

I was sitting on my bed looking out the window when I saw Zion's mother's car pull up in front of the apartment, and Zion got out. I just started crying as I sat there. I didn't leave the room because I wanted him to come in, so he and I can share a private moment.

Zion entered the room, closed the door behind him, and approached me, sitting on the corner of the bed near the window. He knelt, put his head in my lap, and his arms around my waist. We cried together, then we just got in the bed and lay there. I showed him the picture I had. I told him what the doctor thought was wrong with her, but they wanted to see both of us once the arrangements and services were over.

He said he and Momma were going to the funeral home tomorrow to make the arrangements. He was also going to get her a dress. I couldn't think about all that; I was happy he was home, and his mother was so supportive. On the day of the funeral, I was in another place. I sat in front of her little casket; I didn't even look inside. I wanted to remember those eyes looking back at me, not a stiff little body.

A lady at the funeral came to me and said, "You don't grieve over your child." I just looked at her and said, "Why? She is in a better place. If I grieve, it will be for us, who are still having to go through all the madness in this world. I won't have to see her go through. So, if I grieve, it will be for that." I don't even know who that lady was.

We drove to the cemetery. I stayed in the car; I did not want to see the dirt on the grave. Zion saw and knew where her little body was laid; that was good enough for me. If I ever wanted to visit, he knows where she is.

People stopped coming after the funeral. Zion and I needed time alone together to start the healing process. We had to see the doctor who treated Sharmeka; he wanted to tell us what was wrong with her.

We went to the hospital to see the pediatric cardiologist. He told us Sharmeka's heart hadn't completely developed; she had the right side of her heart but not the complete left side. That is why her heart rate could not be regulated. So, our baby died of a real broken heart.

The doctor said, "You can put it that way." The doctor said," He was sorry they couldn't do more, but she would have needed a heart transplant, and the fact that she was so small, the chance of her living a healthy life would be slim to none." We thanked him for all he did and left his office. We didn't want to go, but we both were glad we did; we know now.

Zion stayed home for a month; then he had to get back to the ship. We talked a lot about our future and what we would do after he got out of the Navy, whether he would get out or re-enlist. I didn't want him to leave, but I had no control over that, the US Navy owned him now. I was grateful they allowed him to come home while the ship was at sea. I guess the loss of a child was serious enough.

After Zion left, Junior and I went down south to spend some time with my Grand-ma-ma; it was good for me not to be in the apartment sleeping in my bed at night; I missed talking to Sharmeka in my womb. I missed her even though she was here on earth, alive for one day.

Being at my Grand-ma-ma's, the change of scenery, the fresh country air, walking barefoot in the grass, listening to nature and night talks, and sitting on the porch after a long day gave relief. One of the things I loved doing together was crabbing.

She taught me how to put the chicken meat on a string and throw the end with the meat in the water. The other end had a stick tied around it with a rock holding it down. I had to watch the string to see if it was moving; when I saw it moving, I would slowly pull it until I saw the crab. Then, I would use a net with a long handle, scoop it under the crab, and place it in the bucket; sometimes, more than one would be eating the meat. It was fun and exciting crabbing with my grandmother.

While I was at the local grocery store, I saw my father's wife. She spoke and asked me if Titus knew I was there. I told her I didn't know. Her next question was, "How long are you staying?" I told her for a couple of weeks. She said, "OK, it was good seeing you."

For some reason, I didn't believe she liked seeing me. I felt like she was just being polite because that's what people do here. They may not like you, but they will be nice and polite to you and then talk about you with others. In the small town, everybody knew everybody's business, and very few minded their business. But one thing they did was come together when there were games, funerals, and church functions.

It was nice how the local churches united to support each other's programs. I would go to church with my grandma Tilly; her church was more like my church in New York. My Grand-ma-ma's church was nice but a little stuffy. The people sang old hymns. There was no lifting of the hands praising God out loud, only me when I was there, and they sang about my love, the lover of my soul.

At Grandma Tilly's church, there was hand clapping, foot stomping, hand lifting, tambourine playing, and praising God out loud. They also had a testimony service. Grandma Tilly would be so proud to stand and testify and tell of the goodness of the Lord. And she would say, "I'm so happy my granddaughter from New York is with me today."

Grandma Tilly was tall, dark-skinned, statuesque, and strong-built. She was my Grand-ma-ma's stepmother, who lived next door to her. Even at Grandma Tilly's church, some people would ask me if I had seen my daddy since I was home. I could tell that at some point or another, my father and I were the talk of the town.

The Questions

I made up my mind that this time, I'm not leaving until I reach out to him to ask him those questions that cross my mind every time: he sends me a gift, and when I'm here, I'm not invited to visit him and my other sisters and brothers. I remember Praxton saying, "If you want answers, you have to ask questions."

One morning, I walked down the road to visit our cousin Lawrence, who was in a wheelchair due to a car accident; he lived alone. We became friends. My Grand-ma-ma would send me to his house with food from time to time. Lawrence's front porch faced the road to my father's house, so he knew when anyone would come out of that road or go into it.

While visiting Lawrence, I consulted with him, asking if he thought Titus would really talk to me about not being allowed to visit his house. He said, sure, Titus is a good guy, and he stops by from time to time before he heads home. I told him I was going to call him before I left down here this time. I'm tired of all the rumors and not knowing what is really going on, I need to know.

Lawrence and I talked about the old days of his life. He and my Uncle Ed, who died in a car accident before I could get to know him, told me about the day when my Uncle Ed had just gotten a new Corvette convertible; he liked driving fast. One day, he was driving too fast around a dead man's curve, and a truck crashed into him. Lawrence said that was one of the worst days of his life when he heard about his friend Uncle Ed's death.

My Uncle Mel was married to Lawrence's sister, her name was Sadie. Lawrence wasn't a real cousin. We call everybody cousin so-in-so; everybody was related to somebody, so that made all of us cousins.

We would talk sometimes until it got dark, and I would have to walk back down the dark road to my Grand-ma-ma's house. Lawrence was happy when I told him I had met Jesus and had been saved. He would ask me to pray for him because he knew he wasn't there yet. I would tell him but, "God is here with you, and he loves you." I always left knowing I made his day; he said he didn't get many visitors.

The next morning, I got up and had breakfast. After breakfast, I got the local phone book and looked up Titus's phone number. I found the name and the number. I just stared at it for a while, afraid of making the call. I had to do it. If I didn't, I wouldn't have answers.

While in my thoughts, the phone rang. My Grand-ma-ma answered, and then she called and told me the phone was for me. I picked up the phone in the living room and said hello. I was so shocked to hear the voice on the other end of the phone; I couldn't believe it. "Hey, baby, how are you doing? I heard you were in town. I want to see you; I heard you married and about your baby girl. I'm so sorry.

I was still in shock but heard every word. It was him, my father. I was so quiet he said hello are you alright? I said yes, I was in shock and unbelief that you were on the other end of this phone just as I was looking at your name and phone number, too afraid to call you.

How did you know I was here? Did your wife tell you? I saw her at the store in town, last week. He said no she didn't say anything at all. Lawrence told me. He flagged me down yesterday on my way home. How long are you here for, he asked. He said I will get over there to see you before you leave after I told him I was leaving that Friday; it was Monday at the time.

He said I love you and I'll see you later, okay baby. I said OKAY and hung up the phone. I was so thankful that he called; I knew it was God; God knew I was afraid to call. Thank you, God, for Lawrence.

I loved hearing my father say, "Hey baby." He had such a deep kindness in his voice. I could also hear in the kindness a strong, stern, and lovable man that I wanted to know more about, as well as his family and my family. I knew only rumors about Titus and his family. I wanted to know more about him and his brothers, sisters. My aunts and uncles.

I was excited and wanted the time to come; When I saw his red truck turn into my Grand-ma-ma's lane, he didn't tell me when he was coming, but I was sure it would be before I left on Friday.

After a few minutes, my Grand-ma-ma came into the living room. She asked if that was your father on the phone. It sounded like Titus. I told her it was, and I was surprised and happy to hear from him. My Grand-ma-ma is the quiet type of person, and she didn't prie into other people's business. She knew some of my feelings about wanting to get to know him, and we talked about it occasionally. I told her it was him, and she smiled and said, " Well, I'm glad he called. Is he coming to see you? I told her what he said.

Grand-ma-ma and I spent the next couple of days going around getting all the things, I liked that I couldn't get up north. We had to go to different towns to get some of them. We went to Bogalusa for the best southern smoked sausage, their pickled pig lips then to Franklinton for homegrown catfish.

Each time we left the house, I would pray that I did not miss the red truck or the man who drove it. The days were moving fast. It was Thursday, and no Titus yet; I only had one more day. I began to think he was not going to come.

I sat on the porch watching every car go up and down the road, praying that the red truck would be next. I sat down all morning. By late afternoon, I saw it; I was so excited as it approached the beginning of my Grand-ma-ma's lane. It didn't stop or turn in. It went right on by. My heart sank; my eyes began to fill with tears. God why? He doesn't have to pretend he wants to see me, but he really doesn't.

Just as those thoughts raced in my mind, the phone rang. I picked it up, said hello, and it was him. He said, "Hey baby, I'm at Lawrence's house. I didn't want to stop by your Grandmother's to see you cause people to talk, so can you come to Lawrence's? I'll be there in a few minutes." After I hung up, I asked my Grand-ma-ma if she would watch Junior; I was going to Lawrence's house. She said it was fine and she had something for me to give him anyway.

I walked down the road to Lawrence's house. When I got there, Lawrence and Titus were sitting on the porch. I spoke and gave the bag to Lawrence, my Grand-ma-ma had sent. Titus hugged me and kissed me on the cheek, and in that voice and with the brightest smile, he said Baby, you look good; how are you and your family? How is your mother? I said fine to both questions.

I knew we didn't have much time together, so I asked the same questions and the big one. I said thank you for all the gifts and money you sent me over the years. But why is it that when I come down here, I can't go to your house and see you there and the others? Why can't I call you at your house? Why do we have to meet here?

He said, well, baby, it is a long story. And right now, I really can't take the time to tell you. I want to, though, because you asked, but I must get home. I wanted to see you before you leave tomorrow.

I will get your phone number in New York and call you when you return, and we can talk. And if you need anything, call Lawrence, and he will flag me down. Here is a little something for you and the baby. He gave me some money, hugged me again, and told me he loved me.

As he was about to leave, Lawrence came out of the house from putting the bag away. He said his goodbyes, got into the truck, drove across the road, and down the lane to his home.

I turned to look at Lawrence, and he was looking at me and smiled and said I'm here when you need me 'cos. I told Titus the same thing. I wanted to ask Lawrence why questions, but I needed to hear them from my father. So, I just said thank you. Then I told Lawrence, can I pray for you because I don't have any money to give you? He said sho' I can use all the prayers I can get." I prayed, said my goodbyes, and told him I'd see him in the next round. He said to be safe. I stepped off the porch and returned to my Grand-ma-ma's house without answers.

When I returned to my Grand-ma-ma's house, Ron and Suzanne Titus's oldest children was there, they would sometimes visit and speak to me when I was down on other visits. They didn't stay long, and we had small talk.

I was kind of happy to be going back to NY. I felt a new relationship had started with my father, with a new sense of belonging.

When I returned to New York, I decided to look for a job. I was hired by the City and worked in the complaints department. Lucky me, I get to listen to complaints while, at the same time, missing Zion and Sharmeka. I was able to save my paychecks because Zion always made sure we were good.

I worked with a lady who kept me laughing. She always read dirty, trashy novels and tried to get me to read them. I read one paragraph, and my spirit was convicted. I told her I could not read that kind of stuff. Not to mention,

Zion wasn't home. I didn't need to open my mind to things like that. He would call every weekend when he wasn't out at sea. He wrote to me and told me the ship would be coming in soon, and one of his Navy buddy's wife, who lived in Newark, would be coming to Norfolk to meet the ship when it docked, and he wanted me to come with her. He gave me her phone number so we could connect. I was excited, happy, and ready to see him. It would be nice to meet another Navy wife as well.

We connected and planned to meet in Newark. We would go from there to meet the ship. I was excited to meet her. It was awesome that she knew the Lover of my Soul, too.

The weekend before I was to leave to meet the ship, Titus called me. I was happily surprised. When I heard, hey baby, this your dad, my heart leaped. I said, hey, for some reason, I couldn't say dad. As we began to talk, he said he wanted to answer my questions, and he told me Lawrence said hello. He was calling from his house. I said to tell him hello.

Because I didn't know how much time he had, I went right in; why can't I come to your house when I'm there? Why doesn't your wife like me? Why don't the other sisters like me or speak to me? And why must you send me things through my grandmother or aunt?

He said, hold on a minute; I can only answer one at a time. He said Baby, it wasn't always like that; I don't know if you remember that I would always send you money with Sandra on the school bus when you were younger. One day after you had moved up north, my wife and I saw your mother at the Laundromat in town, and my wife told your mom to let you come over when you were in town. And sure enough, she did; on that day, I came home from work, and there you were, playing in the yard with the other children. They approached me and said, " Daddy, we have a sister. I said yeah, you do.

He said I don't know if you remember that. I don't remember. Titus told me that the next day, his wife's mother had come by, and the children were telling her about you and that they had a sister. I don't know what my mother-in-law said to my wife, but from then on, she didn't want you to come around me or have anything to do with the children. I never denied you.

I asked him if he knew what her mother said to her. She told her that we didn't need to be taking care of someone else's child. After that, it has been a problem whenever you come down or your name is mentioned. Everything was good until my mother-in-law said what she said. I'm sure it was more than she told her. Anyway, baby, that's pretty much it; she ain't backing down after all these years, and she still feels the same way.

I was happy to have some knowledge as to what and why. He said again, Baby, I love you, and you are mine, and no way will I ever deny you. I must go now. I will call you next week. I told him it would have to be the week after because I would be leaving to meet Zion.

He asked how Zion and Junior were. I told him that both were doing fine. I will call you when you get back. Call Lawrence and let him know when you're back. I love you, baby, and we'll talk more then, he said, and we said goodbye.

After hanging up the phone, I began to think back to the time before I would visit my grandmother, and his mother-in-law would always speak and be nice to me at church; she attended the same church my grandmother did, but for some reason, her smile and voice didn't seem genuine. Maybe that is why she would call my grandmother after church, and whatever they talked about would lead to me returning to New York. I still have questions even more now. They will have to wait. I was focused on meeting my husband at the ship and spending time with him.

Reunited Feeling Good

Laura, Zion's Navy buddy Lance's wife, was very nice. We took the bus from Newark to Norfolk. We talked most of the way. She said her husband may not recognize her because she had lost a lot of weight. I didn't know what she looked like before, but she looked amazing now. She had to be about a size 6 or 8. She had blonde hair. She was about 5'7" or more with a very pleasant face. She had some color to her skin tone to be a white girl. She was cool. She knew the lover of my soul, the holy one, and we shared the love of the King of Kings.

Whenever we stopped and there was a jukebox, I would play the song "Reunited" by Peaches and Herb. I longed for his touch and for us to be together.

Once we arrived, we both found our rooms; we had special accommodations as military wives. The next day, we went to the pier where the ship was due to pull in; we were so excited standing there among the other wives, girlfriends, and family members of those sailors, standing at attention as the ship pulled into the docking port and the song blared, "In the Navy."

I tried to see if I could see Zion in the midst of the sea of white starched uniforms, but I couldn't. There were too many, and their hats covered their faces. I was so happy to see the letters on the side of that ship, USS Donald B. Barry. I knew he was here, and we would be reunited.

I said a silent prayer, thanking God that he was back safe and that Laura and I were able to be right where we were at this very moment, waiting for our husbands to come off of the massive ship.

After all the formality of the navy, they let the sailors off the ship. Zion spotted me first, and he grabbed me from behind. He said I know that hair from anywhere. Lance was with him, and sure enough, he didn't recognize Laura, he was looking for someone with a lot of extra weight. She grabbed him and said yes, "It's me". Zion said you don't look the same way you did in Great Lakes, where he first met her during his basic training. Lance just smiled and showed an expression of pride.

They took us on a tour of the ship and introduced us to some of the other sailors. It was so exciting. I didn't care where we went or who he introduced me to. I was with him, and that was all that mattered.

Later, we went to the motel room, where they had to change out of uniform so we could go to lunch, and they showed us around town. Zion said I have been longing for this. We gonna have to do a quickie before we get with them. It was like he was reading my mind. Quickie, it was, but it felt so good to be one again. Now more than ever, I believe that distance makes the heart grow fonder.

We only had the weekend together until he came home on leave in a month. I made sure I brought a sexy nightie for later that night. After Zion and Vance showed us around, we said our good-nights and retired to our rooms. We would normally take a shower together, but I told him to go first because I wanted to make an entrance with my sexy nightie. And I did. Zion was lying on the bed when I left the bathroom, the lights down low. He had his boom box playing "Always and Forever" by Heatwave, one of his favorites.

He looked at me and said girl, you look so good, better without clothes; he complimented me on the nightie and then said you don't need it. I just smiled and said take it off then; you can have it. And he did just that very slowly as he caressed every part of my body the nightie touched. That was it. He had taken it off, and the rest of the night was filled with passion. I could feel all his frustration, pain, compassion, and love that night.

We weren't having sex. We were making love; I felt the difference. I felt no guilt, shame, or like we were doing something wrong. I knew the lover of my soul was pleased. The love was intoxicating; I was so high. I understood the song by Diana Ross, "Love Hangover", because the next day, that is what I had. My body was so relaxed, with no tension, renewed. We both needed each other in that way. I understood the difference for real. It had to be like heaven. He (God) does honor marriage; I felt so blessed.

We couldn't do anything when Zion was home for Sharmeka's funeral because my body and my mind were all over the place. God knows what we need; we need each other. The weekend was very nice. I never liked saying goodbye to Zion when he left to return to the ship. I felt like I was being bounced and abandoned again like when I was a child. This time it was me leaving him.

On the way home, Laura and I didn't talk too much. I think we both wanted to savor every memory of the weekend. We had a common bond. We were Navy wives. Zion and Lance only had less than a year to go before deciding whether they wanted to reenlist for four more years. I didn't want him to, but I knew it was his choice, and I wasn't going anywhere either way he decided.

I had a family of my own, and I loved my husband. And I knew the Lover of my Soul loves us both. I felt His presence so strong when we were together (God's presence). I took Monday off from work; when I returned from Norfolk, it was a long weekend, and I was not ready to let it go. However, on Tuesday, before I could sit at my desk, Ms. Pretty smiled, saying I know you had a good time because you are glowing. Did y 'all come up for air? I smiled and said good morning to you, Ms. Pretty.

Every day for about a month, Ms. Pretty told me I was glowing, and my skin was pretty. She would tell me sex does your body good. I would correct her and say you have sex; we make love, a big difference. She didn't like that too much, because she knew what I meant when I said that to her. I would tell her sometimes about having intercourse without being married to the person you are having it with. I didn't hound her too much about it; only when she would tease me, that would always get her to stop.

I was so happy to have a job. The days without Zion seemed to pass quickly, and the money I saved by banking his allotment check was a blessing. A couple of months had passed since talking to Titus. I was thinking about him when the phone rang; it was him that always seemed to happen. I answered the phone and heard, "Hey baby," this is your dad. How are you doing? I know it's been a while. I said yes, that's okay. We are talking now. I told him all was well with me.

We talked for a long time about my younger years in New York, how I gave my life to the Lord, and how the Lord blew my high. I told him how much I loved Him and never wanted to hurt Him.

He said he was proud of me, and I sounded happy. I told him I was. He shared with me something he wanted me to pray about. He said they were having problems with the youngest girl and wished they would try to get to know me. He said I was like an old soul with wisdom beyond your years.

It's God, I told him. One of my prayers was to have wisdom after I read the story of Solomon, King David's son, in the bible. God asked him what he wanted, and one of the things he wanted was wisdom. That was when Titus told me he couldn't read or write; he said he had to quit school as a young boy to work in the field with his father. I felt sad and thought that not one of his children would try to teach him. I asked him if it would be ok if I sent him the bible on tape and a bible so he could follow along and look at the words to practice. Saying them, seeing them, and how they are spelled would be a start. He said he would love that, I had to send it to Lawrence's house.

After knowing that Titus could not read or write, I began to understand some things, such as why there were no letters from him and why the cards were not signed; he really had to rely on his wife and those around him to communicate anything written. I almost felt sorry for him.

We talked for over an hour. He said he would pay Lawrence for the call when the bill came out. I asked him to call me once he received the bible and tapes. I was going to send it right away. He said he would and told me he loved me and to take care and give Junior a hug for me. I told him me, too, and we hung up.

I felt so good when I heard his voice. We were talking to each other, and I knew this would not end. After hanging up, I said a prayer for Titus. I wanted God to help him learn to read and write. I thought about how embarrassed I felt when I read aloud in public and couldn't pronounce a word correctly or misspelled words. I can't even imagine being unable to read or write.

He may not be able to read or write, but he is a very smart man and can grow anything from the ground. During one of our conversations, he told me that he grew watermelons for the Federal Government from his nursery. He also owned a barber shop.

A month has gone by since my last period. I think I might be pregnant. I'm almost sure my breasts have been sore, and the lower part of my stomach is harder than usual. I was sleeping a lot, which is a true sign.

I went to my mother's one day after work, and she just came out and said you look like you're pregnant. How does pregnant look when you don't have a big stomach?
I went to my doctor, who confirmed that I was pregnant. I told him I knew when it happened and could tell you my due date. He said March; I said no, April, the middle of April. I did take my pills while visiting Zion; I guess they didn't work.

I was happy about the news, but I was also fearful. I didn't want to have this baby die, too. I knew I had to dismiss those thoughts right away. God gave me peace, and Zion will be home by the time the baby comes.

When I told Zion the news that he would be a father again, he was so happy. Junior was happy and couldn't wait. When I told Ms. Pretty at work, she said I knew it; you glowed when you came back from your weekend with your husband. The job was not stressful, and it was a sit-down job, which was great. Ms. Pretty spoiled me with any kind of food I wanted.

The months went by very quickly. Zion decided not to reenlist in the Navy despite the reenlistment bonus offered. I was happy about his decision because I didn't like saying goodbye when he would have to leave for months, being out to sea. He only had a few months left until he would be home for good and in time for the baby's birth.

It seemed like all the young couples at church were having babies simultaneously. I loved my church; we were like a big family. I learned so much about the Lover of my Soul and how to trust Him. I think I was the youngest on the prayer team; when they would go out and pray for the sick and shut-in, I was among the elder women, laying hands and praying.

The church's mother, who was strong in her faith, would teach the young women how to dress and conduct themselves. I remember when I was new to the church, still wearing my makeup and loud lipstick. She taught me how a woman of God should dress. She knew I was grateful because I wanted to do everything right and not hurt the Lover of my Soul. I took everything off. I felt bad that I didn't like what I saw in the mirror, so I told Mother Gloria, and she said, "Baby, if the Holy Ghost in you doesn't convict you, neither do I.

You must look in the mirror before leaving home and ask yourself and the Holy Spirit if this is okay. Let the Holy Spirit be your guide." I was thankful she did not judge me or condemn me.

I removed the blush and foundation, kept my eyeliner, and softened the lipstick color. Most of the women did not wear makeup. Well, none of the women wore makeup or pants. I was the only one. Mother Gloria didn't want my clothes to rub off on the other young ladies. Going to church and being involved in its activities was also a way to learn more about my Lord and Savior and keep my mind off the time away from Zion. We had service on Friday night, Sunday morning, afternoon and evening. It didn't seem like much to me because I felt Him there and enjoyed being with others who loved Him.

The singing and testimony service I enjoyed the most. One of the sisters I met at the church could sing heaven down. I believe heaven would tell the angels to hush and listen to her. Rene was truly anointed; when she sang, it was from her soul.

The testimony service was nice because not only did the older people testify, but the little children did, too. They would stand up independently; some would sing their little song and tell how good God was to them. I was amazed because they were so sincere. I was also happy to have Junior be there to see it.

Junior was very shy. I knew it would take him some time to warm up to the other children and begin to share something God had done for him. He loved watching Oral Roberts, and I knew it would be a matter of time before he would sing their theme song and share the testimony of his healing

Junior and I prayed together every morning and at night. I wanted him to know the Lover of my Soul. If I couldn't give him the world, at least I wanted to give him that knowledge. I wanted to live a life that he would not be ashamed to say I was his mother because there were times when I hated my mother was my mother. God has changed all of that. I see her in a new light now, I see her through the light of Christ.

I joined the church choir; I would get so caught up in the words of the songs with my eyes closed and hands in the air; the choir director would remind me in rehearsal to keep my eyes open and on him so I would know what he was directing us to do. He knew he would have to remind me again. It was my spirit reacting to the words of praise to my savior. I didn't know how to control it; there was a fire, a ball of love for Him I wanted to express for Him openly.

My spirit was so alive in Him; my body didn't know what to do. Sometimes, I felt like I would leap out of my body. I wanted to. My body was holding me back. I knew there was more to my being. I could feel it. But it was also more than a feeling. It was an unexplainable wholeness. I could hear Him; I could see Him in everything.

When I would throw my hands in the air, and my mouth would praise Him, it would get stronger and stronger. It was a natural high that nothing in the chemical world had ever given me. I wanted everyone I knew to share this high, but most would say it doesn't take all that, or they would say I was faking or being phony.

I will testify sometimes, telling them if they see or hear me doing something wrong, please correct me because I did not want to go to hell through the church. I had already seen a glimpse of it and wanted no part of it.

Zion came home about a month before I was to have the baby. I was happy that he didn't have to leave again and that he was going to be with me for our baby's birth. It didn't take long for him to find a job. He was hired at one of the major companies, which paid well and bonuses. I was still working at city hall. We were a working couple not waiting for a welfare check; our children would see us work to take care of them.

We were in a good financial place, so we bought a car off the showroom floor, a Chevy Chevette four-door with a hatchback, navy blue. We also talked about buying a house. I wanted to wait a year to give us time to have a larger down payment for a home with everything we wanted. Not to mention that where we was living the rent was $79.00 a month, with everything included. We could save and get just what we wanted in a house.

Zion didn't like that the building had roaches even though our apartment was under control. I had dealt with them for so long; what was one more year? I knew we would pay more than $79.00 monthly for rent or mortgage. We could be good for a long time with both of us working. He wasn't hearing it, and they weren't helping with the rent. Roaches or not, I thought one more year and we could be sitting pretty.

He still wanted to move and find a house. Maybe it was because he was raised in a home, not an apartment complex. We are looking for a house.

The morning my water broke, Zion had ridden his bike to work and took the car keys with him. My cousin Lee and her husband lived in an apartment around the corner. I called her to see if they could take me to the hospital; after talking to her, I called my doctor and Zion's job.

Lavelle, my cousin's husband, had to stop and get gas for the car. The car always needed gas. I don't think Lavelle ever had a full tank of gas. And I didn't understand why Zion took the keys to the car with him to work, knowing this could happen any day. Lavelle dropped me off at the door to the emergency department and drove off. I think he was nervous.

After I was checked in and on the labor floor, the pains started. They checked the baby's heart rate and me to see how many centimeters I had dilated. Once they confirmed everything looked good, I could walk around to help the process move along faster. I was hoping Zion would make it in time. Why would he ride his bike? He would have to ride home, leave the bike, then get the car and come to the hospital. Of all the days he knew it could happen any day, I am sure he had his reasons.

The pain was becoming more unbearable, and there was less time between them. As I was standing in the hallway leaning against the wall, waiting for a contraction to end, I looked up and saw Zion rushing down the hall toward me. He grabbed my hand and asked what he could do to help me. I just wanted to go back to my room to the bed. I knew he was nervous because he asked the nurse to bring a cool towel for my forehead to remove sweat when I wasn't sweating. I told him to put it on his forehead. He seemed to need it more than me.

An hour or so went by the pains didn't seem to break in between. I asked the nurse to call the doctor because I think I felt the baby's head and I was having a lot of pressure. She did. When the doctor checked me, he said yes, we are ready to have you push.

They moved me to the delivery room. Zion was holding my hand, then looking to see the baby come. I didn't care how he handled it all. I was just happy he was there. I gave about three good pushes, and out came my baby boy, six pounds, seven ounces, and twenty-two inches long. Zion's face was lit up like a Christmas tree. The pride and the fear of being a father were all over him. He also had a look I couldn't figure out. It was almost a look of awe.

I was happy the pain was over, and my baby was here. I didn't want him out of my sight. I thought if they took him away, something might happen to him. I asked them to clean him up and check him over, and they did. Then they gave him to Zion to hold. He brought him over close to me; I only saw his nose and lips. I told him, "Baby, I'm sorry; I slept with your daddy."

He looked just like his father. He was bright-skinned like me. Zion was so excited; I just looked at him with gratefulness. I thanked God for him being there and a healthy baby. I was married, and I knew this man loved me. Junior has a little brother. His playmate.

I wanted to name him after Zion's father, Thomas George the Third, but Zion said no, and he named him. I was very protective of the baby while in the hospital. I was not going to leave without him. They had to explain everything they did to him in front of me. I'm sure it was because of Sharmeka. I left the hospital with my baby.

Zion had everything ready for me when I got home. He even went out and bought me a beautiful rocking chair. I loved it. Junior was so happy. He wanted to know how long before he could play with him. I told him he must grow some.

My sisters and brothers would come over to see and hold the baby, but when Zion was home, he didn't let them. My little sister, Bobbie, would be so mad at him.

Tyrell was a month old when I took him to my job to meet the people I worked with. When the mayor saw him, he said, "What a fine-looking baby, and those fingers so long he is going to be a piano player." I said you think so.

After my six-week check-up, I was cleared to return to work. I didn't want to go back. I wanted to stay home and take care of my new baby. Zion wanted me to stay home, too. But I wanted to replace the money we used for the car. My mother watched Tyrell while we worked. Junior was in school.

We were a happy little family. Zion was going to church now, too. We had Tyrell christened, and one of his uncles and aunts were made his godparents. I was so happy. Not only did I have my family, but I also had my church family, which God had given to me. However, every time I spoke to my father, Titus, I felt like I was missing that piece of family.

After some months passed, we found a house. While waiting for the process to close and move, I met a young woman who worked as a temp on the job.

We were having lunch together, and she shared with me that she had two children, a girl, and a boy. She was also married but needed to find a place to live because she and her husband were separated.

She said it wasn't safe for her and her children. When I got home later that day, I asked my mother if she would allow her and her children to stay with her until we moved into our house, and then she could take over our apartment. My mother said yes; she was always willing to help someone when they were in need. I told Zion about the situation, and he said that it was a good idea if she went for it.

The next day at work, I shared with Linda the idea, and she accepted the offer. She started to cry. She said why would you do this for me? Your mother doesn't know me. I told her my mother will help you get back on your feet. She loves helping and seeing people make it, especially mothers with little children. No, I don't know you, but my God knows you very well, and if He told me not to help you, trust me, I wouldn't. She began to express she knew Him too. That was it. We prayed and talked about how good God is.

When my mother met Linda, she instantly fell in love with her. I think it was because she looked like she could be her daughter. She had hazel eyes and light skin. She had a country-girl way about her. Linda and my mother got along very well. When the time came for her to move into our apartment, my brother-in-law came to help move us and Linda. When he saw her, and she saw him, it was over. I told her even if you and your husband aren't together, you are still married, and you had better not break the Lover of our Soul's heart. And I said no more to her about it.

Zion and our little family were in our new house across from a school, making it convenient for us and Junior. It was a three-bedroom house up and downstairs, and the bathroom was big. I think that is why Zion liked it so much. I wanted a house with everything on one floor, but we bought the first house we saw because we rushed into buying it. I was happy to have our own home, though. I think we were the youngest and first couple in the church to buy our own house.

One of the things I liked about the house was the closed-in porch in the summer. On warm nights, we could sleep on it, and it was used as an extra freezer in the winter. The house was in a quiet neighborhood; it only had two black families, and we were one of them.

We moved into the house in October of 1980; Tyrell was six months old, and in January of 1981, President Ronald Regan cut the program I was working through with the city, and I could no longer work full-time for the city. They kept me on call and when people went on vacation. It all worked out. I was able to be home with Tyrell more and help Junior with school. Zion was doing well at his job; he was making enough to take care of all the household bills.

I was no longer around the corner from my mother, and I missed being close to my brothers and sisters; they still called me whenever they had an issue. My sister, who was three years younger than me, was trying to take my place by having the younger ones respect her. She and my brother Z would fight constantly, and I would get called to put out the fires.

Zion didn't like that I would run to their rescue. He didn't understand; they still needed me. My mother wasn't always there even when she was. She would let them work it out themselves or say they'd better stop until they break something or hurt themselves. I loved her, but I did not like some of her ways.

Zion would tell me you have to let them figure it out for themselves. But he didn't know sometimes they didn't know how to do that, and I would need to go and just be present. They loved and respected me. They missed me not being around the corner and within walking distance. I know I did.

They were my blood, and I was their sister/mother. I prayed for them daily that God would pour His love and protection over them. I wanted them to know Him. My mother didn't go to church or pray with them. I believe that will change someday.

I had my little family, and Zion wanted all my attention. I loved to see Zion come home after work and play with Tyrell and Junior; he seemed proud. Junior would let Tyrell do anything to him; he was just happy he wasn't alone anymore, and he had his little brother, who, to him, could do no wrong.

As Tyrell got older and got into trouble, Junior would tell me not to whoop him, but he wanted to take the whopping instead. That got old after Tyrell was always going to get a whopping'. Then Junior would say, "Ma, whop him."

As the boys got older and a few years passed, I noticed Zion didn't want to attend church with us anymore. He was working trick shift, so I just took it as if he was trying to get his body in line with the changes, but he also became agitated with some of the little things we did.

I missed him going to church and the time we would have fellowship with the other couples. Zion and his friends, some of the brothers, started a singing group; they could sing. When they practice, the wives hang out together. Zion even bought himself a base guitar. He didn't know how to play it. I enjoyed watching him try. He would call himself teaching the boys sometimes. I would be like, "You can't play?" How are you teaching them to play?

Now, his job consumed him. I would call my grandmother every weekend. It was always refreshing to hear her voice. I would ask her questions about raising children. She would tell me to enjoy them while they are young, "they may be on your apron string now, but when they are older, they will be on your heartstring." They won't stay young forever; one day, you will wish for this time.

She told me that every time she saw Titus in town or somewhere, he would ask her about me and tell her to say hello, saying that he loved me. The little girl in me just wanted him, not those words but I was grateful to hear them anyway. I would just say okay tell him the same.

It was getting close to summer, and our down south family and Aunt V had planned for a family reunion in the south. I was home preparing for the trip when I looked outside across the street at the school and saw a police car, which was odd because our neighborhood was quiet. I thought no more about it and went on with what I was doing until the phone rang and it was the school's nurse. She said I needed to come to the school where Junior was in her office. I began to have all kinds of crazy thoughts after seeing the police car there.

Red Ants

The day before, Zion told me the school had called and said Junior was poking kids with a fingernail file, and he whipped him. Junior had baseball practice later that day, and I noticed he was walking slower than usual. I asked him if he was okay, and he said yes. As much as he loved baseball, he wasn't himself. I thought it was because he had gotten in trouble for what he did in school.

When I got to the school, a police officer met me at the door of the nurse's office. He began questioning me about the incident yesterday, asking me if I knew my husband had beaten my son. I told him my husband told me about it and that he whoped him for poking some children with a nail file. Then he asked me if I had seen the bruises that were left. I told him I had not. He was old enough to bathe and dress himself.

The officer walked me into the nurse's office, where my son was standing with his shirt off. When our eyes met, I could see so much fear and pain when he turned around for me to see his back, when I saw the bruises from the top of his back down his legs, some open blood-dried thick whips. I cried, "Oh my God, Junior, I'm so sorry." All I wanted was to go home and kill Zion, especially when they told me Junior didn't poke the kids; he was motioning as if he was poking them. I wish I had gotten the call because I would have asked more questions about the incident.

The officer told me that the child protective services would come to my house later that day and that I should take my son home. I told them I didn't know the extent of this and would confront my husband.

On the way home, Junior told me he went to the nurse because sitting down was hard for him, and the teacher sent him to the nurse's office. I let him down because I didn't protect my son. My heart was bleeding; I prayed when Zion got home that I didn't take a knife and stab him to death; who does something like this to a child? Maybe it was because he wasn't really his son, or he took all the frustration he had been going through out on Junior.

All kinds of thoughts were racing through my head. I hugged Junior and told him I was so sorry this happened to him, but it will never happen again. I promise you that. I didn't hold him too tight because I knew it hurt him. He went to his room and lay down. I went to my room to pray.

God, what am I going to do? I need you to help me, show me what to do. That's my baby, God, that's the joy of my heartbeat. I love him and Zion; how can I be in this place; he wounded my son, and I see the emotional wounds of my husband. Guide me, Lord. I need peace in my mind to make the right move. I don't want to move in this anger and pain I feel. HELP! Only you can bring healing and peace.

Zion came into the room while I was praying. I stopped and looked at him. He could tell something was wrong. I asked him, "Do you know what you did? Did you see Junior's body? He said I told you I whopped him for what he was doing to the kids in school. The school called me to come over because Junior had to go to the nurse's office. He couldn't sit down, and his clothes were sticking to his body because of the bloody wounds, and the police said child protection would be coming to the house.

I told him he needed to look at Junior and see what he had done. When he looked at Junior, tears welled in his eyes, and he looked in horror, shame, and pain, like he couldn't believe he had done something like that. He then took Junior to the bathroom and began to nurse his wounds, apologizing repeatedly as he nursed him.

At that moment, I saw a different person in Zion. I felt pain for both my son and my husband. I knew child protection was coming to the house. I couldn't let them take my son away from me. I don't want to lose my family. But I pray Zion understands that he can't touch Junior again. Zion left after he nursed Junior's wounds; child protection came not more than five minutes after he left.

It was a middle-aged white woman. She came in, looked around, and sat in the big-armed chair while I sat on the couch. She began asking questions about Zion and whether he had ever done this before. I told her no and promised her it wouldn't happen again. She said she would need to talk to him, and when she does, she will let us know her decision and what would happen next. I told her we were preparing to leave for a family reunion. We would not be back for a week. She said she would wait until we return to complete her investigation. She looked around again as I walked her to the door, then she left.

It never failed that every time I saw the sign, Folsom, my little girl's heart would jump because I knew I was closer to my daddy. I told Lawrence to let Titus know my family and I would attend the reunion.

I loved seeing my grandmother and being in the South. I felt at home. I walked around barefoot most of the time I was there. It didn't matter that the ground was hot.

My mother did the same; she walked around barefoot, too. The feel of the ground, the earth, you knew was a part of your roots, and it was soothing.

Grand-ma-ma's house was full, and everybody was doing something to prepare for the reunion. Aunt V did most of the cooking. There was so much food that looking at it made you sick or hungry. The children were running around in the yard, and the men were gathered under the big pecan trees in the yard firing up the grill for the meats to be grilled.

It was the first time Zion met my down-south family. I couldn't help watching Junior while he was playing with the other children. I could tell he was still sore. He seemed to enjoy his cousins; he'd met for the first time.

I dare not say anything about what happened. My uncles and other family members would not be kind or forgiving, and my mother would want to kill Zion. He promised he would not do it again. So, after meeting him for the first time, I didn't want them to dislike him.

Tyrell was about two years old then, and I enjoyed watching him run around trying to keep up with the older children. He loved to explore things until he explored a red ant pile. The ants weren't happy and left bites on him to ensure he never explored them again.

The reunion was wonderful. I met so many great uncles and aunts. I enjoyed talking to them about their lives and when they were growing up. There was so much history I never wanted to forget. Cousins from all over the North and the South; new relationships started. This was my mother and grandmother's side of the family. I couldn't help wondering what my father's side of the family was like.

The day before we were to leave, I met Titus at Lawrence's house. I asked him about his brothers and sisters. His father was still living, my grandfather. He told me about his mother, whom I met as a little girl; his brother, who told me to call him Uncle Prent, took me to meet her. She had my school picture on her wall. I was surprised to see it. I remember her smile.

I asked Titus if his wife still felt the same. He said she does, and every time my name is brought up, it's an argument; that made me sad. He told me the next time I would come down. He will see if one of my cousins can take me to New Orleans to meet his brothers and sisters and their children. Our visit ended as always; he gave me some money, hugged me, and said, "Baby, I love you, and don't forget that, okay." It always felt good to be in his arms. I felt the love he had for me.

Later that night, as the southern sun went down, we were all sitting on the porch, talking: my grandmother, uncles, aunts, and my mother. My uncle asked me if I had seen my father. I told him I had. My mother said, "Is Tessie still acting crazy?" I told her I called her to find out why she didn't like me, and she said, "I need to talk to you."

My mother said I didn't want to be with Titus, and I told her she could have him. What does that have to do with me? We both were friends at one time. She believed that I said, Miss Dotson, that someone else was your father. Miss Dotson took me to the hospital when I was going to have you. She even named you. Tessie's mother told Ms. Dotson that I said you were her granddaughter. I told her I know whose daughter you are. Ms. Watts was your godmother. People talk.

I told my mother I just needed the truth. I'm hearing too many different stories. Why are you all not willing to come together and have a sit-down when everyone is here at the same time? That would put an end to all the talk. My mother just repeated, "I know who your father is, and I don't have to prove anything to anybody."

I could tell she was getting uncomfortable. So, I didn't say anything else. But my Uncle Beard said your mother did crazy stuff when she was pregnant with you. She drank rubbing alcohol and tried to drown herself, crazy. My mother got up and left the porch. She was agitated. I could tell there was something painful she didn't want to reveal.

On my way home back to New York, I thought about everything that had occurred mainly my mother's reaction to our conversation. I felt in the pit of my gut that there was way more to what was not being said.

Zion drove most of the way back, making it easier for me to recall the trip's events. Back to my life and family matters here. The Monday we returned, the child protection lady came to talk to Zion; I had almost forgotten. Junior seemed a lot better. I could tell he didn't see Zion the same; there was a caution about the way he acted around him, which I thought was understandable.

About a week goes by when we get the phone call from child protection that the case will be dropped and sealed; if they receive anything else from our home, the children will be taken, and Zion's name will go on file as a child abuser. I praised God for their decision and that my children wouldn't be removed.

I was beginning to see the high cost of having my own family. As the years passed and the boys got older, we prayed and read the Word of God more and more together—the boys and me. Zion hardly ever prayed with us; he would say, "You all go on and pray."

Zion was a good provider monetarily, but we walked on eggshells emotionally. We didn't know what would set him off. We had wonderful days and horrible days. He was upset one day with Tyrell about what I can't remember, but in the midst of his ranting, he told Tyrell that he was worse than a maggot and wasn't worth the skin he was in.

I jumped in and told him not to destroy our son's spirit by saying that. It didn't stop him; the verbal abuse was insane. Words can kill you. Later, I would tell Tyrell that you are worth more, and he is just angry at someone or something else and taking it out on us.

I was willing to sacrifice my sanity and my children's emotional sanity for my family; the price was high. I knew the navy had changed Zion in ways he would never tell me, but his actions spoke volumes.

The good days were so good you almost forgot the bad; they were so bad they left all kinds of scars. I will not forget that I love Zion and pray for him to be delivered daily. But the verbal abuses, the yelling, and the ranting were only slowly ripping a hole in my heart.

I would talk to my grandmother, and she told me it is better to deal with the devil you know than to get with someone you don't know. I didn't want to leave Zion or divorce him. I wanted him to get help.

I believed the Navy did something to him, and he needed to be deprogrammed. I felt like we could work through anything with God's help. I knew God honored marriage. I also believed Zion loved me and the boys. He just needed help he wasn't allowing himself to get.

Sisters

My baby sister moved in with us during her final high school years. I was grateful she helped with the boys since I had been working. She fell right in place with us; the boys liked her being there. She would go to church with me and the boys. She made new friends there. They would come over for Sunday dinner from time to time, go skating, and go to the movies. I was happy she liked going to church.

She told me she loved hearing me pray every morning. I would get up before everyone else so that I could spend time with the lover of my soul. I needed our time. He is my peace, joy, and everything. There were times when, and if it had not been for Him, I knew I would be insane. I wanted my sister to know Him, too. I took the opportunity to visit my grandmother, and while my sister was there, she stayed with the boys.

On this trip, I met and stayed for a night with Sandra, Titus's oldest daughter, so we could talk. I had questions I hoped she could answer. I took the plane straight from work. The dress I was wearing must have been in the washing machine for a while before going into the dryer. I could remember it smelling like mildew. I thought I was about to get with my sister, oh God. When she picked me up, I got into her car.

I could tell she smelled it. She drove with the windows down and the air conditioner on. When we got to her apartment, she said, "I'm sure you want to shower after that long trip." I did. She had planned for us to go out and meet some of her friends. We did, and I had a nice time.

After we came back to her apartment, we talked. I asked her why Titus' other daughters didn't like me, and she told me it was because every time my name came up around the house, their parents would argue. That's when Sandra said, "It wasn't that I didn't like you;" I just thought you were trying to play on both sides of the fence because I heard you were someone else's daughter. That's when she began to tell me about this one day while I was visiting my grandmother, and Otis's daughter came to see me.

Rumor was that he was my father, an old school friend of my mother's. She thought it must be true and that I was trying to play both families.

Sandra clarified how much she loved her mother and didn't want to hurt her. She loves her dad and didn't want to hurt him either. And not to mention, they say you're not his. At that moment, I couldn't hold back any longer. I'm not asking you to choose. You are grown now. I had to let her know that I was hurt by the painful words she said. And, in rebuttal, I blurted it out to Sandra. "They say the same thing about you, that you're not his," She said, "It's the only dad I know," I told her the same here: You just happen to live with him.

As badly as I wanted to be a part of their lives, I couldn't wait until the next morning when she would drop me off at my Uncle Jonas' house so he could take me to my grandmother's. Before the night ended, her mother called, asking her why she had me there. I was hurt and angry. What is it about me that they don't even want me in their presence? I may be grown up now, but I am still the child in this matter.

The next morning, when I got out of the car, I told her thank you for everything and that I would not bother her again. When I got to my uncle's house, I cried—so hard. I could tell my aunt, and uncle didn't know what to do or say.

Once I got to my grandmother's, just seeing her eased the pain. Uncle Jonas stayed for a while, long enough to eat the meal that grandmother had prepared for us, something she always did when someone was coming home from afar.

After he left, we sat on the porch talking. She asked me how my visit with my sister was. I told her the story and that she did not want me as her sister or that she was not going to choose sides with her father or her mother. My grandmother said it's just a shame how some people can be. All this happened before Tessie's time. Grand ma-ma said don't worry too much about it. God will work it out.

While we were talking, the phone rang. My grandmother answered and said it was for me. The voice on the other end eased the pain even more, especially when I heard, "Hey, baby, how are you doing?" It was Titus. He told me he heard I was by Sandra's house, and his wife was not happy about it. I told him everything we talked about and how sorry I was for blurting out of pain to Sandra that you weren't her father either.

Titus began to tell me all about what happened. He said he promised his mother he would not leave his wife, Tessie.

She said I was the father of the baby she was carrying, so my dad made me marry her. And my mother said, "Once you bring the baby home, never deny her." He said, "Baby, I will never deny you either. I feel you are mine more now than ever." He said, "His sister Tee's daughters will be coming to take me around to visit his brothers and sister. They want to meet you."

The next day, one of the daughters called to set a time to pick me up. She came mid-morning. We went to Franklington to see my uncles and their families. As I met more of the family, I felt like I belonged. I looked like them, and I could see some of my ways or their ways in me.

Helen took me to New Orleans to meet family there, too. I had a wonderful time, and they treated me like I belonged. One of my aunt's daughters introduced me to blue Bell Banana Pudding Ice Cream. I was hooked. We had fun that day, which made up for the start of my trip.

I told my grandmother about everyone I met; she was happy for me. We talked and sang some of our favorite gospel songs. I only saw Titus at church that Sunday. He spoke but very briefly; his wife was nearby watching. I told him I would be leaving the next day. He said he didn't think he would be able to see me again before I left. The little girl in me cried inside. I hoped one day, all this would change.

After church, I stopped by my uncle and aunt's house, my grandmother's brother and wife. We talked until the sun went down. He told me stories of him and Grand-ma-ma growing up and how he was protective of her.
He gave me one of the birdhouses he built. My uncle was very bright-skinned, soft-spoken, and kind.

He told me he helped to build the Causeway Bridge. It was amazing to me to know that someone in my family helped to build the longest bridge in the world. He also told me about his conversion, when he accepted God into his life.

He said he used to run around and play the field but was tired of it. He was getting dressed to go out when he heard the Lord's voice. He knew he wasn't living right, so he said, "I just stopped doing the wrong things. I was going to be committed to my Lord and my wife."

All his children were successful and married with families, and he became a great role model for them. We had talked so much that I didn't notice his wife had left the room. I left my uncle's house enlightened and filled with more understanding of some things he and my Grand-ma-ma had to endure.

I wished I had a father like him when I was growing up. I had to pack everything up when I returned to my Grand-ma-ma's. I didn't know how to get the birdhouse home, but I was. My Grand-ma-ma packed it up for me so it could be checked on the plane. Uncle Jonas came over later to drive me to the airport the next day. Once again, I didn't want to leave. I knew I had to get back to my family.

Bobbie picked me up from the airport. As I was greeting her and getting into the car, I heard in my spirit, "Here you have a sister who loves and adores you and always wants to be around you, and you reject her.
Let her love you; she accepts you. While you are looking for love from sisters who don't want to have anything to do with you. You have a sister right here."

God forgive me for not seeing this before. It was like an instant love for Bobbie came over me, a sister's love. I was happy to be home in my bed. Zion was so glad to have me back. The boys told me never to leave them again. Bobbie told me she didn't stay at the house the whole time I was gone, which seemed strange, but I dismissed thoughts as to why.

Love's Blanket

I told Zion all about my trip and how I met some of my father's people. I also showed him the birdhouse my uncle gave me. The next day, he put it up in the backyard and filled it with birdseed. He didn't say much about me meeting my father's people. I felt as though I was alone in this father thing, and if anyone understood, it would be Titus.

No one who had and knew their father and mother could ever understand the empty, lost, and abandoned feelings you deal with every day. I know if it weren't for God and His grace and mercy, I would be dead from drugs. And I thank Him for Junior giving me a reason to live before Him. Now it is for Him the Lover of My Soul I live for.

Zion started staying away from home a lot, and when he was home, he seemed to start a fight to have a reason to leave. In the morning, when we would pray before the boys left for school, he would tell us to go ahead without him.

I remember being at lunch with one of the girls I worked with at the bank and telling her how much I loved Zion, that he loved me, and that I didn't think he would ever cheat on me. She smiled and said that was good, and she was happy for us.

Later that same night, I got a phone call, leading to some news that changed everything. My heart was crushed. I could not believe it, but when I confronted him, he said he was high, and the drugs were the influence. I didn't know what to do.

He kept apologizing, saying he didn't want to lose me over his stupidity. God, what do I do? I can't trust him now; I didn't want to lose my family. He promised it wasn't going to happen again, and he would only get high on weekends.

I prayed and knew that because of my love for God, I had to forgive him, even though I didn't trust him anymore. I still loved him. God, help me!

It was hard to look at Zion without thinking about it. I didn't want to see or hear his voice, but I wanted to. A part of me thought I was going crazy. The Lord would always remind me of a passage of scripture that would bring me back to Him. "Keep your mind stayed on me; I will keep you in perfect peace," or "Think on these things" were some of the words I would hear. Also, "Love covers a multitude of sins." I knew God had forgiven me, and I had to forgive Zion.

This is a pain I had never felt before, the pain of betrayal. Sometimes, I would think of Jesus on the cross, and he asked the Father to forgive them because they didn't know what they were doing. Then I would tell myself Zion knew what he was doing, and if he truly loved me, he wouldn't want to see me hurt. All the ranting, the anger, and the beast that came out of him was enough to deal with. Something was lost in our relationship that I don't think will ever be found again.

Titus called me briefly after this happened and kept asking me what was wrong. He said my voice had changed; he didn't hear the usual joy and light. I tried telling him without telling him what was wrong.

He got it. He said Baby, forgive him and save your marriage if you love him. Without him telling me, I knew he was in the same situation. I had heard things and remembered how this nurse looked at me when he took me to see his father in the hospital. I knew something was up.

He encouraged me to give Zion another chance. Then he said, "Give it to God; he'll help you work it out." I was thankful for the advice and heard his voice on the other end of the phone. The little girl in me wanted to be curled up in his arms, my head lying on his chest, feeling the security of those words. I said, "Thank you; I will try." He said he was going to pray for us, and we said goodbye.

I asked God to help me see Zion in a new way, and to move on from this, and see that I could forgive him and let it go. It took some time for Zion to rebuild his trust. I had to trust God for Zion, not put my trust in Zion. My trust was in God because He honored marriage.

The boys were older; they saw and felt the change in me and Zion; we were on two different paths.

One morning, on my way to our church's prayer meeting, Junior yelled from his room that his girlfriend was pregnant. I told him to stop playing; I didn't have time for this. Junior was about to graduate from high school and maybe go off to college. Tyrell was in middle school now. Time was not standing still, and neither were the boys.

I met Junior's little girlfriend one day when I came home early from work. She was coming down the stairs in my house.

I asked her, "Does your mother know where you are?" She said, "Kind of." I said, "What does that mean?" she said, "I'm supposed to be at volleyball practice. "I replied, "My house doesn't look like volleyball practice; what is happening here? What ball, or shall I say volleyball, you are practicing on here?" I was so upset, mainly with Junior, because he knew I told him not to have company in my house when we were not home and to treat young ladies like they were his sisters.

Well, that didn't happen. Now, he is telling me she is pregnant.

I told that little girl that day as I walked with her down the street, "Junior wasn't ready for a serious relationship, and you should value yourself, especially your soul." She didn't listen. Now, I'm going to be a young grandmother. This was a lot to take in.

Being a young mother made it almost impossible for it not to happen. I made my mother a young grandmother. I am sure my Grand-ma-ma was a young grandmother, too.

Once Zion and I accepted that we were going to be grandparents, we sat down with the girl and her mother to let them know we would help in every way we could. Junior was present as well. I could tell Junior was happy and afraid. He was on his way to a possible football scholarship from Penn State.

The recruiter from Penn State came to the house to talk to us; all was going well until the recruiter said, "We like to make sure the player has family support; can we count on that from you?" I shook my head and said, "Yes, most definitely," but Zion said, "He can't keep his room clean, and I won't support him." The look on that man's face said it all. Not to mention that it ended the visit. We never heard from him again.

Tyrell said, "I'm going to have a famous brother." I don't think he understood the impact Zion's answer made. I was so upset with him. I asked him what his room had to do with being his parents and supporting his dream.

During our going back and forth, I realized he was jealous of me and the boy's relationship. I told him years ago that the boys would be older one day if he didn't spend quality time with them and me. We will look at each other and say who are you? I was at the schools, at the games they played. The boys and I prayed and played together. Yet I was still a mom, not only to them but to some of their friends. Junior's friend Nate became my other son. He would come early some mornings before school to join us in prayer and get a hug.

Missy, Junior's girlfriend and now the mother of my first grandchild, was an only child. She was a beautiful girl who still had much growing to do. Her mother was charming to meet, and I was happy that we all worked together for the best interest of all the children (Junior, Missy, and Baby).

On the day of the baby's birth, Missy's mom and I were walking down the hall of the hospital. I told her we were about to meet our granddaughter. She said no grandson. I told her maybe next time, but we are having a granddaughter. After processing and accepting that I would be a grandmother, Missy became a part of the family. I wanted her to have a girl. I would talk to Missy stomach.

I prayed and asked God for a girl because I wanted my son to think about and know how precious a man's daughter is to him.

When I would talk to Missy's stomach, I would tell the baby to kick if it was a girl and not if it was a boy. The baby would kick every time I said girl. I talked to her every time Missy would come over. When the baby was born and I went in to see her, she was crying, and I said, "Hi honey, we finally met." She instantly stopped crying and started looking around. I believed she knew my voice. She looked at me with those beautiful eyes; she looked like my son but bright, like her mother.

Junior was so emotional he was crying. I hugged him and prayed he would be a good father, being so young. When Junior graduated from high school, Zion helped him get a job where he now works. He was laid off from a big company he was hired from after leaving the Navy. Junior couldn't take the smell; it was a paper company warehouse, so he went off to college. I knew he wasn't cut out for that kind of work.

That didn't sit too well with Zion. I understood Junior needed a job to take care of his baby. With a better education, he would be able to get a job he would enjoy and make a better living. Journee (the name they gave to the baby) was an infant, and by the time she reached the age of really knowing him, he would be done with college and able to take care of her financially and be present in her life.

Tyrell was happy to be an uncle. I think it made him feel older. When Missy allowed the baby to come over, There was someone younger than he was in the house. I wanted to see her every day.

Being a grandmother gives you a whole new feeling you can't explain. Being the paternal grandmother, you have less say when seeing your grandchild.

I'm a grandmother, and she is here. No matter how she got here, she is beautiful and a blessing. Her other grandmother says she looks like me and her mother, but she looks like Junior.

When my mother saw Journee, she smiled and said, "She's a pretty baby." I could see the pride in her eyes as she looked at Journee. I just thought, "Wow! My mother is a great-grandmother, and I think Journee is also my father's first great-grandchild."

I called Lawrence to let my father know about the baby and asked if he would call me. Lawrence said he would flag him down when he saw him come up the road. "Congratulations to you, Grandma," Lawrence said, then laughed. I said thank you, and we ended the call.

It took Titus a while to call me. He said he had been very busy with his nursery; he had gotten a contract to grow watermelon again for the federal government. It took up most of his time. I said, wow, that is great, and it was okay. I knew there had to be a reason. He said he knew about the baby because he ran into my grandmother in town at the local grocery store; he couldn't wait to see her. Can you send some pictures to Lawrence for me? I told him I would.

He asked if they were getting married. I don't think so. That would have been how I wanted her to come to them being married first. I didn't want Junior to repeat how he came, but I know children are a blessing from God no matter how they come. I said, "Right," implying how I came. He said, "You're right, baby."

He said he couldn't talk long but just wanted to call me and hear my voice. I told him, "Same here; I wanted to tell you about being a great-grandfather." He said, " Wow, great grandfather." Alright, baby. I look forward to that picture. I love you. I said I love you too, and we hung up. Once again, questions and feelings about why we have to communicate like this were raised. I dismissed the thoughts and was grateful to hear his voice.
It just so happened that my baby sister Bobbie had her baby four months later.

I was there with her in the labor room, wishing she was having a boy. As soon as the baby came out, I said it was a boy, But the doctor said it was a girl. My sisters asked which one it was. It was a girl, so I proudly cut the umbilical cord.

The baby turned blue, and as they rushed her out of the labor room, I stopped them, laid hands on her, and prayed life into her. She was lifeless, but God! She didn't cry and was not breathing as they rushed her out of the room. I am sure my sister was concerned.

I trusted God that she would live and not die. And she lived; my sister named her Alexandria. She looked just like my mother. My mother was so proud to have a new granddaughter, great-granddaughter, and goddaughter in the same year. There were three beautiful baby girls. My friend from work, who was living with my mother at the same time my sister was pregnant, was pregnant with her daughter and named her Tayler, my mother's goddaughter.

The Nightmare

When Alexandria was about four months old, my mother, sister, and my son Tyrell took a trip south to my grandmother's. I spoke to Titus to let him know Tyrell was coming and that maybe he could meet him. And maybe he could go to the shop to get his haircut. He told me during the conversation that he wished his wife would try to get to know me because maybe I could say something to help with their baby girl. She was giving them some trouble. I said I would call her again, and now that my mother is going to be there with all of you in one place, maybe the truth can come to light. He just said you can try.

Once my mother arrived, I waited a day or two before calling Titus's wife. I called and said, "Hi, how are you? This is Raelynn." She said, "Oh, how are you and your family doing?" I said we were doing well. I told her I was calling to ask if you would be willing to set the record straight about me and who my father is.

My mother is there now. She said she knew who he was; she said Titus was my father. I told her I have a grandchild now, not to mention my children can't just spend time with their grandfather. I think it's time for all this to be put to an end. She said, "I heard you were a grandmother now. Congratulations." I said thank you.

She went on to say, "I'm not going to talk to your mother. I believe what was told to me, and you look more like him than you do, Titus." She said, "Raelynn, I don't mean to sound mean, but this has all been a mess, and you are like my worst nightmare. You are like wearing a wet overcoat in the summertime. I'm sorry you don't know who your father is, but I'm not going to talk with your mother."

My heart sank; I felt like nothing. She said to, me, the innocent child in this grown-up mess, I was her worst nightmare. I told her that was serious, and I felt sorry for her. I said, "I am going to pray for you." I thanked her for her time, said God bless you, and hung up the phone.

I knew I did not need to talk to my mother again about talking to her. I can't believe they used to be good friends. My mother and uncles would tell me they were classmates and were very close at one time, which is hard to believe now.

Theresa called to tell me that they were enjoying Tyrell's visit. He was having a good time with her brothers hanging out riding their four-wheelers, and it was good that he was getting to know his other family. Titus also called to tell me he had a rough night the day I called. He said his wife wouldn't let him sleep, and she cried all night. I felt so bad for him.

He said he saw Tyrell and that he had cut his hair. He said he was so happy to meet him. Tyrell told me he met his grandfather and asked why he had so much gold in his mouth and if he was rich. That is when I told Titus what Tyrell had said. And he was happy to meet his grandfather. I said it's so sad that we must do things secretly. I pray one day, this will end. He said me, too, but he didn't know what it would take. He said he would never deny me as his child. He felt like I was his, and he loved me as his daughter; that was all that mattered to him.

I appreciate that, but this mess is happening in a new generation. I have grandchildren now who will never know you or your side of the family. He said, "Baby, I don't know what to do." I said, "Let's pray about it. I believe

God will lead and guide us." He agreed. We prayed on the phone and said our usual, "See you later, and I love you." I knew all I could do was trust God to do what we couldn't.

I was in so much inner pain. I wanted to talk to Zion about it. I wanted him to hold me and tell me everything would be okay. But over the years, I stopped confiding in him. When he was in his moments of rage, he would throw stuff back in my face. I went to my secret place in the closet in my hallway and cried out to God. I couldn't understand why an innocent love was forbidden, the love of a little girl for her father. Some say I should move on and get over it; you're grown now; it shouldn't matter. It was easy for them to say.

They were the ones who grew up with a mother and father or at least one of them. They knew who they were and where they came from. They will never understand. I was holding onto an emotionally and verbally abusive marriage for the sake of my children, not having what I didn't. The lover of my soul honors marriage, and he hates divorce. I may have hurt them by staying rather than helping them. Their relationship wasn't a good one. The boys didn't know what to do when he would come home from wherever. We didn't know what would trigger him or his mood swings.

I loved Zion, and that didn't change. I still believed he loved me. I prayed that he would give his life to know God's love and peace. After all, our church was born out of his mother's living room. I quickly learned it doesn't matter if you were raised in the church. If the church wasn't in you, then you are not truly living the life God wants you to live. If it wasn't for the Holy Spirit, I know I couldn't live this life. No matter how much I go to the church building, he is our helper.

I was so grateful that God saved me the way he did that night in my apartment. He has kept his promise. He has never left or forsaken me, even amid all I have been going through.

My mother, sister, and Tyrell made it back from down south. Tyrell told me all about his time down there, how much fun he had with Therese and her brothers, and that he went to Titus' barber shop and got his hair cut, and Titus brought him back home to great grandmama's and gave him $20.00 for ice cream. He went on and on about the trip and said he couldn't wait to return. I was happy to hear the excitement in his voice about the trip. Sad about the situation

Tyrell, I'm glad you had fun and met your grandfather. I said as I interrupted him. Then he said, "Ma, he got a lot of gold teeth. I said I know all of them do him and his brothers. When they smile, all you see is gold. Their father did, too. As he lost his teeth, he would keep them in his pocket. I thought that was funny.

I remember visiting Titus's father in the hospital in Covington. Titus took me, and that is when he showed me his teeth. I laughed because he said, "Nobody was going to steal them." He flirted with all the nurses. He was funny to me, and we had a great visit.

Titus told him if he kept that up, they were going to put him out of the hospital. He told me I look like them. He called me a pretty little thang, "Baby, there ain't ugly Howard's."

I said it like he would have said it to Tyrell and me. Tyrell said, "Sho' ain't not from what I have seen so far."

Tyrell asked if he could go and spend the summer with Titus some time. I just said, "Maybe one day, we'll see." I didn't want to go into all the drama with him. Another innocent child was affected by all the drama.

I knew something needed to be done but didn't know what to do. My children are getting older. I'm getting older. It is time for this madness to stop. Our church's conference was coming up, and we will be fasting before it; I'm putting this before the Lord. The fast was for three days. It was hard on the first and second days. I wanted to give up, but I was too close. I repeated what Jesus said in Matthew 17:21, saying that this kind only comes out by fasting and praying.

I told myself you only have one more day. The third day was wonderful with the Lord in our secret place. I didn't want to come out, but life doesn't stop. I still had to cook, care for the house, and go to work. I would imagine what it would be like outside my body, spirit, and soul being with him always. I wanted to feel his presence.

Tim Storey was the guest speaker at the Holiday Inn Conference Center. I will never forget his message. He spoke about Moses carrying the children of Israel out of Egypt and how he carried them spiritually. I remember him calling me out of the hundreds of people, and bringing me on stage he asked me if I would be willing to carry my family out of bondage.

I said yes, and he then prayed over me and for me. As he prayed, I felt very light and an inner strength I had never felt before. I also felt a new peace. I saw someone helping me off the stage floor when I opened my eyes. Tim then said to me, "Go! Deliver your family." I didn't know how it would be done or what it meant, but I had peace and strength for whatever was to come.

Soon after the conference, I read an article in a magazine at my doctor's office about blood tests and DNA. I thought maybe Titus and I could do that to end the issue of who my father was. Maybe we can finally get the truth.

When I got home from the doctor's appointment, I asked Zion what he thought. He said I should do it. I had written down the phone number from the article, so I called to get more information and find out what I needed to do.

They told me it cost $450.00 and that they have centers nationwide where you can have your blood drawn. I asked them if it mattered that the other person was in another state. They said no. All they needed was the person's name and address, and once paid for, they would send each person the information on where to go. I was excited I could get some closure. The blood doesn't lie; people do.

I called my mother and told her I would ask Titus if he would be willing to have the blood test done. Why did I do that? She said, "I know who your father is; Titus is your father. I wish you would stop this! Leave it alone!" I said no one wanted to tell me the truth when everyone was there (down south). At the same time, I asked if you all would set the record straight, but no one was willing to, except Titus.

Mother, I have a grandchild now. Don't you think this has gone on long enough? She just said, "Do whatever you want to." Then I asked her, "Is there anything I should know?" She just repeated, "I know who your father is," and hung up on me. Her reaction made me more determined to go through with having the test done if Titus was willing.

The next day, I called Lawrence's house but did not get an answer. I must have called all day, but no answer. I didn't have any other way of getting a message to Titus, so I prayed he would call me. I was concerned about Lawrence.

A week went by, and I had a dream that I was down south visiting my grandmother. I was walking down the road to Lawrence's house. When I arrived, he was not in his wheelchair but standing on the side of his house, working in his garden, which he'd planted. I was so happy for him. I said, "Look at you." He just smiled at me and said, "Yeah, girl, God is good." I think your prayers worked.

He said, "I just keep the chair as a reminder and a witness." Then he turned and continued to work in the garden. I said, "I've been calling you." Then I heard my son say, "Ma, I'm ready." It was Tyrell waking me up to pray before he left for school. I was kind of disappointed that the dream seemed so real. I wanted to know why Lawrence didn't answer his phone.

Later that day, Titus called me. I was so happy that my prayer had been answered. He told me he called to tell me that Lawrence had died. My heart sank. I said I knew something was wrong, and you won't believe it. I just had a dream about him last night or this morning. I told Titus about the dream, and he said Baby, it was almost just like that.

I went by his house and saw the wheelchair on the porch where he would be sitting. I had helped him start a little garden on the side of the house. He said he would let me know about any arrangements. He said, "Baby, this hurt me to my heart. Lawrence was a good guy and our only way of staying in touch."

I said I was calling him last week to have you call me; now I know why there was no answer. Then I prayed God would lead you to call me. But I wasn't expecting this. He said, "I know. What did you need?" I said, "Now more than before. Let's do what I'm about to ask you if you are willing to do it." He said, "What's that?"

"Would you be willing to have a blood test done? Maybe it will put an end to all this." He said, "Is that what you want to do? Are you sure?" I said, "It's time for truth; my mother says you're my father; your wife says she was told I'm not yours. I'm just tired of all the secret stuff. I want to spend time openly with you when I'm down there. I want my children to be able to know you and your family. Lawrence is gone now! Wow, Lawrence! I will miss him. I believe the dream was him letting me know he made it and that he is with the Father."

Titus asked, "What do I need to do?" I told him I would pay for it, and they would send the information to your house, where to go, and what to do. I need your address. He said, "Ok," and gave me the address. I said, 'I know you will have to tell your wife; I just pray you don't have to deal with too much." He said, "Don't worry about that. I want you to know that no matter what, you are mine. I love you, baby." I said, "Thank you for that; I love you too. I'll call you when the papers come." He said, "Okay, love you, baby," and hung up.

After we hung up, all I could think about was Lawrence, the talks, and my prayers for him. I was happy I was able to share time with him; he really was a good guy, even though some people in the town just saw him as a drunk in a wheelchair.

The next day, I called the number for the information and where I needed to send the money for the DNA test. I was told I would have it within five days after payment was received. I called Bobbie and told her what I was going to do. She said mother had already told her, and she didn't seem so happy. But you should do what's best for you. I'm with you.

When I got the paperwork, I waited for about two months before I sent it in. Aunt V called me and said, "Are you sure you want to do this? What if it doesn't come back like you want it to?" I told her it was time for the truth, and I would have to deal with whatever. Titus has been dealing with his wife on this for over thirty-plus years now. If for nothing else, he needs peace.

Bobbie told me that my Aunt Em was against it, too. It was hard for me to understand why the pushback. My mother said she knew who my father was, and they all told me that Titus was my father, so what's the big deal?

There was so much push that I had a dream that I was trying to cross the Upper Falls Bridge, and just as I was halfway, a huge blizzard started, and I could hear my family members yelling from the other side, telling me, it's too bad you can't make it. But I pushed through to the other side, where the sun shone brightly, and their voices stopped. I filled in the papers and took them to the post office when I woke. I took the dream as a sign to keep going.

About two weeks later, I received a letter from DNA Diagnostic with a time, date, and place to have my blood drawn. Titus called me and said he got his letter, too. The day came, and on my way to give my blood, I stopped by my mother's house.

I told her I was on my way to give blood and asked if there was anything I should know before I did this. She looked straight at me sternly and said, "I can't wait until the test comes back, and I wish I could see Tessie's face. I know who your father is." I said, "Okay, I'm going now." I felt sure that Titus was my father, and we would soon put every doubt to rest.

I got to the lab at the address they sent me. I walked in and up to the information desk. My heart started racing, butterflies were in my stomach, and knots were in my throat. The lady at the desk asked my name and for my ID. She said to have a seat, and someone would be with me soon. I sat down and prayed, "God, please!"
Then my name was called. The lab tech took me to a room in the back, explained everything to me, took my blood, labeled it with my name, put it in a plastic sealable bag in front of me, and told me it would go out tonight. Depending on the other person giving their sample today as well, I should get the results in a week or so. It's done; no turning back was my thought as I left the lab.

When I got home, Zion was already home from work. I told him I had given my blood today for the DNA test. He looked at me and said, "How do you feel?" I didn't know how to answer because I didn't know how I felt; my feelings were everywhere. He said, "I hope you get the answer you want." Then he called me to come closer to him and hugged and kissed me. That moment felt like him before the Navy, a caring hug.

I needed that from him. He said, "Let's go to the prayer room." I had cleaned a room off from the living room, anointed it, and dedicated it to God for prayer and meditation. I wouldn't allow anyone in there if they did not mean business about prayer. When you stepped into that room, you could feel the change in the atmosphere. I was kind of surprised he wanted to go in there. He avoided that room and even said it didn't make sense.

We just sat on the floor, and no words were spoken out loud. I could feel God's presence so strongly, and I knew Zion could feel it, too. After a while of just sitting, he said, "Okay, let's go out and get something to eat." I was grateful for the moment. I had the Zion I knew from years past; it was nice.

Titus called me the next day and said that he had gone and given his blood. His wife took him; I figured she would have to because he couldn't read or write well. He said, "Well, baby, all we must do is wait and see. I love you, and nothing and nobody can change that."

I told him that if by chance the results come back and I'm not your daughter I will not continue our relationship because I want you to have peace in your home. The only way we will continue is you would have to do it. He said, "Baby, let's wait and see. Be strong." I said, "I know this is probably the talk of town." He said, "Yeah, they talking." I'm sure. I'll call you when I get mine if I get them before you. Ok, baby, we'll see.

Every day after we gave our blood seemed extra long. My family was silent as if everyone was holding their breath.

No one called me. My mother didn't call me to take or go with her anywhere, just silence.

I checked the mail every day. On Saturday at the end of the second week, Zion had left to go fishing, and Tyrell wasn't home. I slept in. Junior was away at college. I did my usual morning prayer and devotion and went downstairs to fix myself some breakfast. It was already past the time for the mailman to have run, so I decided to check the mail. When I opened the box, there it was—the only letter in the box.

My heart was pounding so loudly that I could hear it outside of my body. I had told Zion I would open it with him when it came. I held it for a long time. I put it down and picked it up repeatedly. I tried to fix my breakfast, but I was no longer hungry. I looked at the letter on the table with the big letters D-N-A, which was all I saw. I remembered Zion went fishing, meaning he may not return until late tonight.

Lord, forgive me, but I can't wait. I got a knife out of the kitchen drawer, picked the letter up off the table, sliced the top open, took the letter out, slowly unfolded it, and began reading it. My name and Titus's were at the top; they had graphs and dots I didn't understand. As I got to the bottom of the letter and read, the only part of the letter that shouted to me was 0.00% unrelated. I read it again and again. I couldn't believe what I saw; maybe I had read it wrong, but there was still no change. The words were the same.

I screamed from my soul and said, "Holy Ghost, keep me. Please, Holy Ghost, keep me. Oh my God, my God help me! God, please, please, please help me! Why God? Why?" They all lied to me all these years. "Why? Holy Ghost, keep me!" I was sick; I didn't know what to do. I wanted to die.

My spirit was screaming," Holy Ghost, keep me!" (My soul was ripped to pieces. The pain was so great it shook the very core of my being. I felt like I was going to lose my mind. I was going to go insane. All kinds of thoughts raced through my mind. They lied; my mother lied. My grandmother lied to me. No wonder no one wanted me; no wonder I was bounced everywhere. Where do I fit in this complex puzzle of life? What is family? Who do I belong to?

Oh my God! Why? Help me, Holy Ghost. I went back upstairs and got back into the bed, covering my head, and cried uncontrollably, praying to be kept. I felt myself slipping away into an unknown place within myself. And so many voices were screaming at me. But my spirit continued to say, "Holy Ghost, keep me!" Sleep came and quieted my soul for about an hour or so. When I woke up, I thought about Titus. I knew I had to call him.

I got up and washed my face. My eyes were puffy and red from the crying, and my face looked different. Something inside of me changed the look on the outside of me. The lies I'd believed to be the truth now shook my being.

I went back downstairs to call Titus. I had left the letter on the table. When the phone rang, I wanted to hang up. I didn't want to tell him the results, but we had said we would call one or the other depending on who gets theirs first.

The Blessing

After two rings, he answered the phone. He said he was home alone and about to go into the shop. I told him I had received the test results and read them to him. I couldn't hold back the tears.

He was silent; for a while, I couldn't hear him breathe. I could hear the pain as he said, oh my God, baby, are you alright? I can't believe this. I don't care what that paper says; you are still mine. You hear me? For the first time in all the times we talked, he called me by name. He said listen to me; I have been loving you as my daughter for all these years, and no paper or anything else will change my love for you in my heart. And like I told you; I am still your father no matter what.

I just cried and amid the tears. I said it hurt so much. He said, it does, but I want you not to forget I love you, and nothing has changed for me. I said I'm going to keep my word. I will not continue calling or anything now that the results are here and show you are not my biological father. I want you to have peace in your home.

He said, "Baby, I'm glad you got them first. When my letter comes, I'm going to let her get it, and we'll read it together, then we will call you." Then he asked, "What is your mother saying? I don't want to talk to her or anyone in my family." He said, "Baby, you have to hear what she has to say."

He said, "Baby, I am so sorry I am not there to hug you. I just said I'm sorry, too. He said he had to open the shop, and someone was coming to get their hair cut. He said, "I love you, remember what I said. I said I love you too, and

I'm so sorry you had to go through all these years of unrest because of me. He said stop, don't worry about me. I'll call you when the letter comes. I said OKAY, and we hung up the phone.

I called Mama T, Titus's sister, we had become very close. She was also waiting for the news, and so were the sisters in New Orleans whom I had met and come to love. When she answered the phone, she said hey baby; I just came out and told her I'm not his daughter and burst into tears. She said you are still ours. Something must have gone wrong with that test because you look too much like us for it not to be so. I could hear the sadness and concern for me. The knots in my throat would not allow me to talk too much.

I said, "I just wanted to let you know. I'll talk to you later," and then hung up the phone. Later that evening, Zion came into a dark house and found me on the floor motionless, holding on to the post of our canopy bed. I was moaning; the letter was on the floor in front of me. He picked it up and read it.

Then he stooped down and hugged me, saying I am so sorry, Raelynn, please don't do anything to yourself. How did he know I was thinking about taking the shotgun out of our closet, putting it under my chin, and blowing my brain out so the voices would end? For some reason, he kept saying, "Raelynn, please don't hurt yourself."

Then he picked me up and told me to lay in bed. I didn't say anything. I just laid there. I lay there for two days. Junior came home and came into the room and said, "Ma, are you alright?" He looked at me, I guess, to see if I was breathing. Then he walked away and said, "You're going to be alright." He didn't know anything yet.

I also called Bobbie the same day I called Titus and Mama T. I told her I would not be speaking to anyone other than her in this family and that I didn't want to talk about them.

I finally got out of bed and took a long, hot bath that felt so good. After getting dressed, I went downstairs. As I reached the bottom step, my phone rang. It was Titus and his wife on the line. He said Baby, we got the results and Tessie said, "I'm sorry to say that Titus is not your father." She didn't know we both knew already. She said I should not have tried so hard to fit into his family and shouldn't have sent him all those little trinkets and cards I sent.

I listened to her for a while. Titus was quiet; he didn't say anything. I could tell she felt so satisfied and in her glory. When she mentioned how Titus and I would sneak and do things behind her back, I had to say something. I said, "Tessie, I would like to ask you to forgive me for everything I did, said, or thought about you. I would like to let the record show that in all of this, I was the innocent child."

I was told from childhood that Titus was my father, and that is what I believed. Now, as for the little trinkets and things I sent him for his birthday, Father's Day, and Christmas, I'm sure you did the same for your father, that is, if he is your real father. There is so much junk going on down there. I'm sure everybody has been sleeping with everybody. I was not the other woman having a relationship with a married man.

I was thought to be his daughter, and all I ever wanted was time with the man I believed to be my father, and it was only when I was in town. But as I said to Titus, now that the results are in, it states that I am not his biological daughter. As I said, I will not be calling or sending any more trinkets as you called them. Titus said he still accepts and loves me as his, but from now on, if our relationship continues, it will be on him.

I'm sorry for any trouble or unrest I may have caused in your life. Please forgive me." Titus said nothing. She said, 'Thank you for that and take care." That ended the call. I thought, "Why didn't Titus reinforce his still being my father." Why didn't he say I told her that and said right then what he said to me? It's on him now. Who knows what she said before the call? I'm sure he is in pain, too.

Later, my Aunt V called me and said she heard I got the results back and that Titus wasn't your father. Well, you said you wanted to know. They say my father isn't my father, but I keep going. Out of respect for my God and her, I didn't just hang up the phone; I just listened, and when she was done, I hung up. Was this delivering my family?

Bobbie called and asked me if I would go somewhere with her. I told her I would. I needed to get out of the house. When I got in the car, she looked at me and asked, "How are you doing?" I replied, "Not good." She said, "I can see that." As she drove, I noticed we were going in the direction of Mother's house. She said she had to stop by Mother's first. I wanted nothing to do with her. I didn't want to see her or hear her voice.

I told her okay, but I'm not leaving the car; I have nothing to say. She pulled up in front of Mother's house, exited the car, and said she'd return. I sat there for about fifteen minutes before she came to the door and told me to come in for a minute. I told her I was okay to wait in the car. She was persistent, so I surrendered, went in, and sat on the steps near the door. I could see my mother and Bobbie standing in the dining room.

My sister said to my mother, "You need to tell Raelynn something." She just said I need to leave it alone because Titus is her father. Bobbie said, "No, Mother, he isn't. The test came back that he wasn't." She said, "They're wrong. I don't know why Raelynn had to go and do this. She needs to leave stuff alone."

Bobbie said she had a right to know, and if you don't tell her the truth, you are going to lose her forever. My mother then began to talk about how hard it was back then, how they didn't listen to children when they told them things that would happen to them. As she began to share more, Bobbie motioned me to come and sit at the table. As my mother started to sit, I came in and sat halfway in the chair.

I lifted my head to look at her and hear what she said. Her face had changed, and her eyes began to fill with tears. It was like she went back to that time and place. In the late fifties in the Deep South, she said, when I was old enough, I had to babysit my younger brothers and nephew. My mother was working for a white schoolteacher, caring for her two children. We didn't have much, and black people had to go in the back door of stores and drink from different fountains. It was a hard life for us. My mother had left our father while I was at school and later came back and stole us from him. I was a daddy's girl.

Then she said when she was a teenager, there were a lot of rapes that were just pushed under the rugs. When it happened to me, the man would come in through the window; he smelled strongly of liquor. He put a sock or something in my mouth and a knife to my throat and told me not to say a word. I was screaming inside but too scared he was going to kill me. I didn't fight; I just laid there.

Then she began to cry uncontrollably, repeatedly saying no one believed me when I told my mother what was happening because it was more than once. They said I was a liar because I told them it was a close relative. I don't know if that is why they didn't believe me, but I told my mother the truth; I just became a liar.

Titus and I were talking then, too, but when he started drinking, I quit him. The smell made me sick. Not long after that, I found myself pregnant. I tried to kill myself; I tried to take the baby out of me.

One night, I was walking to the river to kill myself; I prayed, and I saw an angel come to me and say, "The child you are carrying is blessed. I am the father."

But my family always accused someone else. I never wanted to remember those times again, so I just went along with what they were saying. I knew I was with Titus at the same time all this was going on, so that's what I believed.

I just sat there feeling no sympathy for her at all. I still felt she should have told me this before now. Looking at her, I could see a sense of freedom as a veil was lifted from her face. I saw a light over her face, like a new person had been released. Bobbie was crying. I was trying to let go of the pain to show her love, but the pain was overpowering my love for her. We sat at the table for a few minutes, and no one said anything.

Then I told Bobbie I was ready to go. Bobbie told Mother thank you. I looked at her, and she looked at me, not saying a word with her mouth, but her eyes said it all. She said, "I feel your pain and am so sorry." We left and got into the car. Bobbie said, 'Wow, I'm so glad you came in, Raelynn; you needed answers I couldn't give. Mother needed to release all of that." I said, 'She could have done it sooner. "Bobbie said, "Come on, Raelynn. All of this helped her be free." I didn't care at that moment. When she said that,

I remembered what Tim Storey told me at the conference: "Are you willing to carry your family to freedom?" I said, "Yes, is this it, Lord? It must be, and freedom isn't free."

After Bobbie dropped me off at home, Zion told me my grandmother called. I called her back. She said she was checking on me, and she heard about the results. She asked, "What did your mother say. I told her everything," and she then said to me that the brother of the person who molested my mother molested her. Are all the truth and hidden secrets coming out now?

She started to say did you talk to your father but caught herself and said, Titus. I told her I did; he got his letter, too. She said, 'God knows what He is going through; you will be alright." I said, 'I hope so it's not feeling like it now." She said, "You will. Be strong in the Lord." I said, "Grand-ma-ma, I'm alright. I love you; pray for me." She said she was, and we'll talk later.

Zion didn't know what to say or do for me. He just waited for me to say something or make a request, if any. He watched me because he thought I would do something to myself.

During the next couple of weeks, I received calls from everybody telling me how sorry they were or that the test didn't matter. I think something went wrong because you look just like that man. I was shocked to receive a call from Titus again. He said, "Hey baby, how are you doing? I wanted to know if you talked to your mother, and if you did, what did she say?" I told him everything.

He said, "Baby, I believe her." I remember the time, and I knew the guy she was talking about; we worked together. He said he was the nicest guy until he drank. He would get something from the drugstore and put it in his drink. This made him a different person.

He told me Cooper was his name, and his uncle shot and killed him because he tried to do something to his old lady. Titus also told me about Cooper's son, who had once asked him about me. When I was visiting, he saw me at the store in town with him in the truck. I told him you were my daughter from New York. He asked me if I would give him your phone number. Think about that if you two would have gotten together. All I said was WOW! I don't remember that.

Yeah, baby, I believe your mother, but like I said, "You're always going to be mine, and I love you." I said, And like I said- "You will have to continue the relationship." He said, "I love you; don't forget that." Then I told him, "I love you too." And that is how we ended our conversation. And we hung up.

I felt that was going to be his last call, even though I prayed it wasn't. He needed to keep peace in his home, so if he doesn't, I will have to understand and let him go.

It wasn't long after Titus's call—maybe a day or two—when Mama T called me and said, 'Baby, we all feel you are a part of this family. If you are willing, when you come down here, me and your Uncle Prent want to christen you as our god daughter. We still can't believe the results.'

I had come to love Mama T and her family. I told her I felt honored and would love to have them as godparents. She said, 'Okay, just let us know ahead of time when you'll be back, and we'll make all the arrangements." She sweetly said, "Baby, you can't turn love off. When you love somebody, you love them." I said, "You're so sweet, thank you. I'll make sure I let you know." I hung up, thanking God for such beautiful people in the world.

As I spent more time in prayer, the pain began to lose its grip. I remember what Tim Storey said to me again. I never forgot the look on my mother's face after being able to release the pain and trauma that had a thirty-year-plus grip on her.

One of my friends from church said to me as we were walking in the mall one day, "Raelynn, my father could walk up to me today, and I wouldn't know who he is. But what I do know is that God had a plan for me to be here, and by whatever means He used to do that, I'm here. I'm here for Him and His purpose and Glory. That's what matters most to me."

After she said that, something inside me snapped. It was like I came to a clear understanding of things. I understood why I was bounced and why my mother couldn't hug me or tell me she loved me. I understood why she watched the movie "The Color Purple" repeatedly, back-to-back.

But the most important thing I understood was that I was here for a purpose and that God Himself was my Father. Jesus is my brother; the body of Christ is my true family. He has watched over and protected me from the conception of life until this very moment.

I also understand that we, not just me, are all spirit beings first, and God is the Father of all creation.

Once DNA's Truth was revealed, the Holy Spirit gave to me in this poem, *"Precious Little Spirit."*

Precious Little Spirit

Once upon a time, long, long, long ago, there was a precious little spirit, and Jesus loved it so.

He wanted others to know, so he gave her a body and a soul and said, "Go."

She landed perfectly in the womb of her mother.

As she grew, she could hear voices all around her head.
She felt pain; someone wanted her dead.

She asked Jesus why they hated me so much.
I'm not out of the womb; they don't even know.
The love inside me, you want to show.

Hush, my child, I heard.
They will know in spite of what they say.

I said, Jesus, it hurts when they reject me.
Just you wait, my little one, you will see.
When the time is right, I will make you free.

One day, something happened to the little spirit's surprise.
She had fingers, toes, a nose, and two eyes.

It's true you did give me a body.
Now, lord, will you make me free?

I felt so much pressure and pain all around.
My space was getting smaller as my head went down.

Oh lord, I cried; I really have skin!

Was that the wind?

I just screamed and cried.
I came into the world not dead but alive.

I looked at my mother. One of the voices I would hear;
I saw in her face joy, pain, and fear.

I said, Jesus, can I show her now?
He said, in due time, my child, and He brushed my brow.

I smiled; it felt good to know
He was still there.
He said He was going to be with me everywhere.

As time went on, I began to grow.
Who were all these people I didn't know?

Jesus would talk to me and tell me secret things.
When my mother would hug me, it felt like angel's wings.

Jesus, I said, Am I showing your love?
He said, it's a start, even in a hug.

Time went on and on; I could walk and say people's words.
With Jesus, I just thought it, and He heard.

There were others just like me, so little and so free.
Not a care, not a worry, just a bundle of love and joy and chubby cheeks to squeeze.

Now that I am out of the womb and free, growing in leaps and bounds with Jesus' love in me.

Those who wished I were dead can now see that Jesus had a plan for this precious spirit that all the world could see.

GOD IS OUR FATHER!

Everything I went through brought me to that understanding and as Moses did, I carried my family to the FREEDOM OF TRUTH.

Made in the USA
Middletown, DE
07 November 2024